Lobbyists, Governments and Public Trust

INCREASING TRANSPARENCY THROUGH LEGISLATION

Volume 1

OECD

ORGANISATION FOR ECONOMIC CO-OPERATION AND DEVELOPMENT

The OECD is a unique forum where the governments of 30 democracies work together to address the economic, social and environmental challenges of globalisation. The OECD is also at the forefront of efforts to understand and to help governments respond to new developments and concerns, such as corporate governance, the information economy and the challenges of an ageing population. The Organisation provides a setting where governments can compare policy experiences, seek answers to common problems, identify good practice and work to co-ordinate domestic and international policies.

The OECD member countries are: Australia, Austria, Belgium, Canada, the Czech Republic, Denmark, Finland, France, Germany, Greece, Hungary, Iceland, Ireland, Italy, Japan, Korea, Luxembourg, Mexico, the Netherlands, New Zealand, Norway, Poland, Portugal, the Slovak Republic, Spain, Sweden, Switzerland, Turkey, the United Kingdom and the United States. The Commission of the European Communities takes part in the work of the OECD.

OECD Publishing disseminates widely the results of the Organisation's statistics gathering and research on economic, social and environmental issues, as well as the conventions, guidelines and standards agreed by its members.

This work is published on the responsibility of the Secretary-General of the OECD. The opinions expressed and arguments employed herein do not necessarily reflect the official views of the Organisation or of the governments of its member countries.

ISBN 978-92-64-07336-4 (print)
ISBN 978-92-64-07337-1 (PDF)

Also available in French: *Lobbying, pouvoirs publics et confiance, Volume 1 : Quel cadre législatif pour plus de transparence?*

Corrigenda to OECD publications may be found on line at: *www.oecd.org/publishing/corrigenda.*

Foreword

Private interests seeking to influence government decisions, legislation or the award of contracts is part of the policy-making process in modern democracies. Lobbying can improve government decisions by providing valuable insights and data, but it can also lead to unfair advantages for vocal vested interests if the process is opaque and standards are lax. The interests of the community are at risk when negotiations are carried out behind closed doors. A sound framework for lobbying is particularly desirable in the context of the financial and economic crisis, where critical policy decisions are taken in short time spans, massive amounts of public monies are spent and rules and regulations for entire industries are rewritten. The emerging OECD principles for transparency and integrity in lobbying would be one of the policy instruments for building stronger, cleaner and fairer economies.

Lobbying employs considerable resources: for example, a record USD 3.28 billion was spent on lobbying at the federal level in the United States in 2008, employing almost 15 000 registered lobbyists. In Canada, their number at the federal level exceeded 5 000. In Europe, the voluntary register of the European Commission, launched in 2008, received over 2000 lobbyist registrations within the first 14 months.

In view of the downside risks of lobbying and the impressive mobilisation of private resources, public pressure is rising worldwide to put lobbying regulations on the political agenda. So far, actual experiences are limited. OECD survey findings show that only six member countries out of 30 that responded to the questionnaire have established rules on lobbying by requiring, for example, reporting on lobbying contracts. However, many countries – from Brazil to France and Korea – are developing or updating regulations to make lobbying more transparent. However, setting standards and rules for lobbying that are fair, enforceable, and that adequately address major challenges is proving to be difficult.

This report is a contribution to the policy debate in countries which are considering to establish a framework for legislation or government regulation on lobbying in the interest of good governance, transparency and accountability. It provides general guidance for efforts at national level although it can also be applied at the sub-national level. A sound framework requires to consider the following building blocks:

- *Standards and rules that adequately address public concerns and conform to the socio-political and legal context.*
- *A legislation or regulation that suitably defines the actors and activities covered.*

- *Standards and procedures for disclosing information that cover key aspects of lobbying such as its intent, beneficiaries and targets.*
- *Enforceable standards of conduct for fostering a culture of integrity by, for instance, avoiding conflict of interest and providing accurate information.*
- *A coherent spectrum of strategies and practices that secure compliance with standards and rules.*

Since "it takes two to lobby", the Public Governance Committee has carried out complementary work on self-regulation by lobbyists and on alternative measures to government regulation. This was done in order to both provide the full range of available solutions for decision makers and to consolidate a guiding instrument. The Committee is also reviewing a related issue, the revolving door phenomenon, as former public officials lobbying governments is a growing concern.

The report was prepared by János Bertók, Head of the Integrity Unit in the Innovation and Integrity Division of the Public Governance and Territorial Development Directorate. Christian Vergez, Head of Division, provided guidance to the project. Special thanks are given to Michael Nelson, then Registrar of Lobbyists in Canada and to Catherine Macquarie, then Vice-President for Public Service Values and Ethics of the Canada Public Service Agency, for co-chairing the Special Session on Lobbying and for their substantive advice. Assistance in the preparation of the publication was provided by Marie Murphy and Karena Garnier.

Rolf Alter
Director
Public Governance and Territorial
Development Directorate

Table of Contents

List of boxes

List of tables

Acronyms

APS	Australian Public Service
BCC	Business Centre Club, Poland
BIP	Public Information Bulletin, Poland
CAD	Canadian dollars currency
CBOS	Public Opinion Polling Centre, Poland
CMA	Canadian Medical Association
CNEL	Council for Economics and Labour, Canada
CRS	Congressional Research Service, US
EU	European Union
EUR	Euro currency
FAA	Federal Accountability Act, Canada
FBI	Federal Bureau of Investigation, US
GAO	General Accountability Office, US
GRI	Global Reporting Initiative
HLOGA	Honest Leadership and Open Government Act, US
ICT	Information and communication technology
IFiS PAN	Philosophy and Sociology Institute at the Polish Academy of Sciences
KIG	National Chamber of Commerce, Poland
LDA	Lobbying Disclosure Act, US
LRA	Lobbyists Registration Act, Canada
LRS	Lobbyists Registration System, US
ORL	Office of the Registrar of Lobbyists, Canada
PiS	Law and Justice Party, Poland
PLN	Polish zlotych currency
RCMP	Royal Canadian Mounted Police
SC	Statutes of Canada
USD	United States dollars currency

Executive Summary

Lobbying: Globalised practices and emerging concerns

Interest groups that make efforts to influence government decisions are commonplace in modern democracies. Lobbyists can **bring in invaluable information** and data for more informed decision making. Nowadays, lobbying is a worldwide phenomenon, and globalisation has established similar lobbying techniques across continents.

Facing the reality of lobbying in government decision making, many countries have established standards and procedures for enhancing transparency in lobbying. However, emerging concerns in more and more societies are **pushing lobbying onto the political agenda**. Lobbying is often perceived negatively, as giving special advantages to "vocal vested interests" and with negotiations carried on behind closed doors, overriding the "wishes of the whole community" in public decision making.

When lobbying reaches the political agenda, policy makers and legislators face the challenge of determining whether to develop standards and procedures for enhancing transparency in lobbying. If the response is yes, a further challenge is **how to choose from available options**, such as legislation, regulation – voluntary or mandatory – or a policy that is balanced, fair to all parties, enforceable and adequately addresses concerns within their own socio-political and administrative context.

Although decisions on developing or updating regulations for enhancing transparency in lobbying have obtained political support in several countries, setting standards and rules for enhancing transparency in lobbying has proved particularly difficult because it can become a sensitive political issue.

Good governance: Enhancing transparency and accountability in lobbying

This report is a review of the experiences of OECD countries to shed light through legislation and government regulation on the "mystery" of lobbying. The report draws upon research from and consultation with OECD member countries and other stakeholders conducted during 2007 and 2008. The results of the OECD survey on lobby regulations, the comparative overview and the country studies were discussed with the officials in charge of designing and implementing legislation and government regulations on lobbying at the OECD Special Session on Lobbying* in June 2007 in Paris. Consultations were carried out in autumn 2007 with government representatives in OECD countries and then in spring 2008 to obtain the views of stakeholders, businesses, lobby associations, trade unions, professional associations, civil society organisations, academics, international organisations and the governments of non-OECD countries with lobbying legislation. The Special Session and consultations confirmed a strong interest in bringing together lessons learned to develop guidance that could support the policy debate. The resulting guidance together with a comparative review of existing legislation and regulations for enhancing transparency in lobbying consist of key parts of this report.

Since "it takes two to lobby", lobbyists share responsibilities with public officials for ensuring transparency, accountability and integrity in lobbying. Consequently, joint efforts to achieve compliance with expected standards are vital, if lobbyists and public officials mean to avoid stigmatisation of the phenomenon of lobbying and make most of its benefit for public decision making. The report promotes the development of a good governance approach and measures through a deeper understanding of **potentials and limitations of existing legislation and regulations** in place for enhancing transparency in lobbying, namely in:

- **Building a Framework for enhancing transparency and accountability in lobbying:** the first chapter presents the building blocks for developing a framework. It provides decision makers with guidance and policy options to meet public expectations for transparency, accountability, integrity and efficacy when considering legislation or regulation for enhancing transparency in lobbying.
- **Comparative overview:** the second chapter reviews key aspects of existing legislation and government regulations and analyses approaches, models and trends to identify a set of building blocks and "state of the art" solutions based on identified good practices.
- **Country experiences** to understand how existing legislation and regulations reflect the socio-political and administrative context is vital. Experience shows that legislation and regulations on lobbying have developed incrementally as part of the political learning process. Country chapters

* The OECD Special Session on Lobbying took place on 7-8 June 2007 in Paris. Further details, including agenda, documents and presentation slides can be consulted at *www.oecd.org/gov/ethics*.

highlight key stages of the evolution of legislation on lobbying over the past two decades in Canada, the sub-national experience in Quebec, and the Polish efforts to improve transparency in lobbying in the law-making process through new legislation. In addition, these chapters outline challenges and lessons learned in implementing legislation, in particular supportive institutional and procedural frameworks and measures for enforcement.

Building a framework for enhancing transparency and accountability in lobbying

Based on lessons learned in existing legislation, the building blocks of the Framework were developed together with officials in charge of **designing and implementing legislation and regulations on lobbying** to offer a practical guidance to decision makers when they are considering development of legislation or regulation as an option. It should not be construed as advocating legislation or regulation as the sole possible option.

The Framework does not aim at providing detailed provisions and technical advice on designing and implementing legislation and regulations. On the contrary, it **addresses a series of interrelated issues that might logically guide the development of a national framework**, including:

- **Developing standards and rules that adequately address public concerns, conform to the socio-political, legal and administrative context.** Proper understanding of the challenge is necessary to develop a suitable policy response: why public concerns pushed lobbying to the political agenda. Clarifying the public's concern – whether it is related to accessibility to decision makers, the transparency and integrity of government decision making or apparent conduct in lobbying – provides decision makers with directions for defining proper responses to address them. Legislation cannot simply be copied from one jurisdiction to another, as they are interrelated with constitutional traditions and rights, for example to petition government, and mechanisms for interest representation and consultation mechanisms, such as "social partnerships". Public authorities have a principal task to **establish standards of conduct for public officials** who are the target of lobbying. Public officials are responsible for ensuring that their contacts with lobbyists are conducted in accordance with relevant principles, rules and procedures, in particular **to ensure impartiality, provide authorised information, enhance transparency and avoid conflict of interest**.
- **Ensuring that the scope of legislation or regulation suitably defines the actors and activities covered.** This is a condition to establish enforceable standards and rules and effectively resolve the mystery of "who is trying to influence whom, how and when" in public decision making. In defining the

scope of lobbying activities, a balance should be reached by effectively taking into account the different types of entities and individuals that may engage in lobbying activities and the need to provide a level playing field for all stakeholders. The primary target is **professional lobbyists** who receive compensation for carrying out lobbying activities, such as consultant lobbyists and in-house lobbyists. However, public concern may demand a more inclusive definition of lobbying activities to provide a level playing field for all interest groups intending to influence public decisions.

- **Establishing standards and procedures for disclosing information on key aspects of lobbying such as its intent, beneficiaries and targets.** Disclosure is at the heart of effective regulation for enhancing transparency in lobbying. Effective disclosure system provides officials and the public with sufficient information to clearly identify lobbying activities. The public's right to know should be balanced however with avoiding excessive demand. This can create a burdensome disclosure system that may collapse under its own weight or could encourage non-compliance. Disclosure requirements at a minimum solicit lobbyists to identify the interest being represented by naming their clients, beneficiaries and their objectives. Effective disclosure system requires timely **registration and periodic reporting** of lobbying activities to provide credible and up-to-date information on what takes place in the world of lobbying. New technologies, in particular electronic filing through the Internet, make possible the collection, processing and dissemination of large quantities of information. However, registration and reporting forms should properly structure disclosed information to avoid overload and facilitate public scrutiny.
- **Setting enforceable standards of conduct for fostering a culture of integrity in lobbying.** Lobbyists share the responsibility for ensuring integrity in lobbying. Self-regulation in the form of professional codes may state ground rules for lobbyists in their relations with public officials, with other lobbyists, with their clients and with the public, for instance to avoid representing conflicting interests. When perceived conduct of lobbyists raises significant public concern, maintaining trust in decision making would require governments to set professional standards of conduct for lobbyists. Then proactive measures for supporting voluntary compliance, for example by providing access to public officials and consultation documents, or legislation could be considered to foster principles of good governance, in particular integrity, transparency, accuracy of information and avoiding conflict of interest.
- **Enhancing effective regulation by putting in place a coherent spectrum of strategies and practices for securing compliance.** Achieving compliance is a particular challenge when governments enter into new fields of regulation, such as lobbying. The Framework therefore outlines strategies and practices for supporting implementation through **communication,**

education, formal reporting, leadership, managerial directives, incentives, sanction and co-ordination. Putting regulation into effect necessitates the involvement of all key actors to establish a common understanding of expected standards in daily practice. Visible and proportional sanctions applied in a timely manner provide "teeth" for effective enforcement. However, adequate institutional arrangements – including administrative independence, capacity and authority – are indispensable for effectively administering regulation, for example by providing interpretation to support daily application, verifying timeliness and accuracy of disclosures to detect non-compliance and take timely action. Good governance requires reviewing implementation and impact of regulation and making necessary adjustments to meet growing expectations of society for transparency in public decision making.

Learning from practice: Comparative overview and country experience

Globalisation has established similar modes of lobbying practices across a wide number of nations, creating common problems and raising similar issues and expectations in diverse societies. However, standards and rules in legislation cannot simply be copied from one jurisdiction to another, as each political system values its intention differently and varies legislative provisions and judicial practices accordingly. Instead, this report supports the **identification of common challenges** and a set of possible options that take into account country context. This caveat is particularly pertinent in Europe, where nations with corporatist traditions are experiencing the tension between two forces, namely:

- the forces of globalisation that established similar lobbying techniques; and
- respect for "social partnerships" that have served them well for many decades.

Each legislature has to review both the need for legislation or regulation and its precise form in the light not only of international experience, but of its own constitutional arrangements and its prevailing political culture. Having identified broad contextual influences on lobbying legislation and regulations, a comparative overview examines the "state of the art" in the field, following a series of questions that might **logically guide the legislation of standards and rules** for enhancing transparency and accountability in lobbying:

- First, who is to be regulated?
- Second, what should they be required to disclose? This is the meat of lobby regulation, and the most difficult to formulate parsimoniously.

- Codes of conduct, in various forms, are addressed by asking how lobbyists can be regulated, and led on to the issue of securing compliance.
- Finally, how can the integrity of lobby regulation be ensured?

Comparative review of experiences in North America, Europe and Australia shows that lobbying legislation and **regulations have developed incrementally**. Requirements in lobby regulation have ranged from registering interests appearing before legislative committees to requiring extensive disclosure of lobby undertakings. Regulatory schemes vary, depending on the cultural and constitutional background of each state. Nevertheless they share more in **common in their approach, purpose, standards for transparency and measures for implementation**. Where transparency and integrity are the principal goals of legislation, effectiveness is best achieved if definitions are broad and inclusive, and the theatre of lobby activities is also defined broadly and inclusively. However, compliance is best secured if definitions, and exemptions, are unambiguous and clearly understood by lobbyists and public officials, practical in application and robust enough to support legal challenges.

Regulation of lobbyists' behaviour has focused on codes of conduct. These establish principles of behaviour – such as honesty, openness and professionalism – and rules to enforce them. Current debate centres on **whether codes should be voluntary or imposed by law**; experience suggests that legislative regulation is preferable. In considering the impact of codes, and other regulatory features of lobbying legislation, it should be remembered that lobby regulation cannot be free-standing. It is part of a regulatory regime consisting of laws, policies and practices that are interdependent and establish the principles of good governance across the public and private sectors.

Any jurisdiction considering the development of legislation or regulation as an option for enhancing transparency in lobbying should not only review their need for standards in the form of legislation or regulation, but also its precise form in light of international experience and its own constitutional tradition. In this report a country chapter provides invaluable insights on key stages of the evolution of lobbying legislation in Canada. After a decade of experience in implementing legislation on lobbying, **higher expectations of transparency and integrity brought lobbying back to the political agenda in Canada** to both strengthen standards in new legislation and powers of the Commissioner of Lobbying in charge of the implementation of the new Lobbying Act.

The issue of legislation on lobbying has also reached for political support in many European countries, from Italy to Central European countries. The experience of Poland reveals how the **scope of draft legislation moved from the original repressive criminal approach to a good governance approach** to promote transparency and accountability in the law-making process. A particular emphasis is given to explain how complementary measures, such as procedures supporting access to public information and consultation mechanisms, promote good governance in the specific socio-political and administrative context.

These country chapters give unique insights including statistical data on implementation measures for putting legislation on lobbying into effect at the national level. The report also **shares experience of the sub-national level**, namely the design, implementation and impact of the Lobbying Transparency and Ethics Act in the provincial level in Quebec.

This report is a contribution of the OECD to support informed policy debate when governments consider legislation on lobbying. Complementary work examines self-regulation of lobbyists and measures taken as alternative options to government regulation to provide full range of available solutions and a consolidated policy instrument for decision makers on increasing transparency and integrity in lobbying.

Lobbyists, Governments and Public Trust, Volume 1
Increasing Transparency through Legislation

Chapter 1

Building a Framework for Enhancing Transparency and Accountability in Lobbying

This chapter presents key building blocks that provide decision makers with guidance to meet public expectations for transparency, accountability, integrity and efficacy when considering, developing, debating and implementing legislation or government regulations for enhancing transparency and accountability in lobbying.

The building blocks address a series of interrelated issues that might logically guide the development of a comprehensive legislative or regulatory framework for enhancing transparency and accountability in lobbying, including:

- *Developing standards and rules that adequately address public concerns, conform to the socio-political and administrative context, and are also consistent with the wider regulatory framework.*
- *Ensuring that the framework's scope properly reflects public concerns and suitably defines the actors and activities covered in order to establish enforceable standards and rules.*
- *Establishing standards and procedures for disclosing information on key aspects of lobbying such as its intent, beneficiaries and targets.*
- *Setting enforceable standards of conduct for fostering a culture of integrity in lobbying.*
- *Enhancing the efficacy of legislation or regulation by putting in place a coherent spectrum of strategies and practices for supporting implementation and securing compliance.*

Summary

Lobbying: A global practice that raises concerns

The existence of powerful interests – corporate, private or other jurisdictions such as sub-national governments – that make efforts to influence government decisions, in particular policy making, legislation or the award of contracts, is a **daily reality in modern democracies**. Lobbying is often explicitly recognised as **legitimate and essential** given the complexity of modern government decision making and the wide impact of government today. Lobbyists can bring in invaluable information and data that can enable more informed decision making and result in more effective public policies.

There are concerns in many societies that lobbying gives **special advantages to "vocal vested interests"** and that negotiations carried on behind closed doors can override the "wishes of the whole community" in public decision making. These tendencies were considered a major threat to public trust at the OECD Ministerial meeting on *Strengthening Trust in Government: What Role for Government in the 21st Century?*[1] Moreover, allegations are often made that lobbying borders too frequently on influence trafficking. This is a potentially damaging trust in the integrity of democratic institutions.

Definition and scope

Lobbying is not a new phenomenon in government decision making. The concept of lobbying goes back many centuries (OECD, 2006a).[2] The essence of **lobbying involves solicited communication, oral or written, with a public official to influence legislation, policy or administrative decisions** (European Commission, 2006).[3] Although lobbying most often focuses on the legislative branch, it does also occur within the executive and sub-national governments as well, for example by influencing the design of development projects and the award of contracts.

Although globalisation has established similar methods of lobbying, actual lobbying practices are deeply embedded in a country's democratic and constitutional setting. For instance, they are interrelated with constitutional right to petition government, interest representation and consultation mechanisms, such as "social partnerships". The findings of an OECD survey (OECD, 2006b) indicated that **no single legal definition** of lobbying is used across member countries. Existing rules related to lobbying reflect particular concerns that they attempt to address in their national contexts.

Enhancing transparency and accountability in lobbying: Good governance approach

While lobbying is widely considered a legitimate activity *per se* across OECD countries and beyond, it continues to have negative connotations in many societies. In order to combat outright abuses, countries have already established criminal provisions against illicit influencing of public decision making, such as trading in influence, bribery and other forms of corruption. **Merely penalising illicit influencing of public officials, however, may not be sufficient to maintain trust** in public decision making.

Effective standards and procedures that ensure transparency and accountability in decision making are essential to reinforce public trust. There is a growing recognition that regulations, policies and practices which require disclosure of information on key aspects of the communication between public officials and lobbyists have become vital aspects of transparency in 21st century democracies to **empower citizens in exercising their right to public scrutiny**. Measures promoting a culture of integrity are also an integral part of the "good governance" approach, particularly those that **clarify expected standards of conduct** in lobbying for both public officials and lobbyists.

Increased public expectations of transparency, accountability and integrity in public life have given new impetus to revisit existing governance arrangements in recent years and pushed lobbying to the political agenda in North America, Europe and Asia, as well as in the European Union. An increasing number of **proposals for legislation** for enhancing transparency in lobbying have been presented to legislators in many OECD countries in order to meet demands that more public light should be shed on communications between public officials and representatives of interest groups. Emerging good practices in corporate governance also encourage voluntary disclosure of participation in public policy development and lobbying of corporations.[4]

Aims and structure

Decisions on developing or updating regulations for enhancing transparency in lobbying have obtained political support in several countries. However, setting standards and rules for enhancing transparency in lobbying has proved very difficult in many cases because it can also become a sensitive political issue. When lobbying reaches the political agenda, policy makers and legislators rapidly face the challenge of determining **whether and how to develop enforceable policies or regulatory framework** for enhancing transparency in lobbying that is balanced, fair to all parties, and adequately addresses concerns within their own socio-political and administrative context.

The Framework is a point of reference that is designed to **support decision makers when lobbying reaches the political agenda**. The principal aim of the Framework is to provide decision makers with policy options to meet public expectations for transparency, accountability, integrity and efficacy when considering, drafting, debating and implementing policies and rules for enhancing transparency in lobbying.

The Framework is primarily designed to help decision makers at the **central government level**. The Framework can also provide general guidance for sub-national level governments to review and improve their governance system for enhancing transparency and accountability in lobbying.

The Framework is intended as guidance to decision makers if they are considering development of strategy, policy or regulation as an option. The Framework should not be construed as advocating regulation as the sole possible option. The Framework does not aim at providing detailed provisions and technical advice on designing and implementing strategies, policies and regulations. On the contrary, it provides a **practical point of reference with policy directions and options** to be considered by decision makers in order to determine whether, and how, to develop strategy, policy and practices or a regulatory framework.

Rather than providing detailed provisions, the Framework addresses a series of interrelated issues that might logically **guide the development of a national framework** for enhancing transparency and accountability in lobbying, including:

- Developing standards and rules that **adequately address public concerns**, conform to the socio-political and administrative context, and are also consistent with the wider regulatory framework.
- Ensuring that its scope **suitably defines the actors** and activities covered in order to establish enforceable standards and rules.
- Establishing standards and procedures for **disclosing information** on key aspects of lobbying such as its intent, beneficiaries and targets.
- Setting enforceable standards of conduct for **fostering a culture of integrity** in lobbying.
- Enhancing the efficacy of regulation by putting in place a coherent spectrum of strategies and practices for supporting implementation and **securing compliance**.

The Framework was developed on the basis of **reviewed experiences** in OECD member and non-member countries that have already designed and implemented regulations on lobbying.[5] They reflect the lessons learned in countries with diverse socio-political and administrative contexts. The Framework was developed in parallel with the *Green Paper of the European Transparency Initiative*[6] and the *Code of Conduct for Interest Representatives* developed by the European Commission as part of its European Transparency Initiative for the supra-national level in Europe.

The Framework is intended to be used in conjunction with existing **OECD policy instruments** and guidance on, in particular:

- Promoting integrity in the public service, such as the 1998 *OECD Recommendation on Improving Ethical Conduct in the Public Service* (OECD, 1998) and the 2003 *OECD Recommendation on Guidelines for Managing Conflict of Interest in the Public Service* (OECD, 2003).
- Enhancing quality of government regulations, such as the 1995 *OECD Recommendation on Improving the Quality of Government Regulation* (OECD, 1995) and the 2005 *OECD Guiding Principles for Regulatory Quality and Performance* (OECD, 2005).[7]

Policies and rules for enhancing transparency in lobbying can effectively address public concern – related to the integrity of government decision making or conduct of lobbyists – when they provide **visible and accurate standards that meet public expectations**. These standards for enhancing transparency, accountability and integrity in lobbying establish the foundation for appropriate conduct, both for government officials and lobbyists. However, attaining compliance with established standards is also necessary, if lobbyists and government officials mean to avoid stigmatisation of the phenomenon of lobbying.

Establishing standards, even in the form of regulation, cannot solve all problems related to lobbying. Effective policies and regulations for enhancing transparency in lobbying should be **well integrated into the wider constitutional, legal and administrative frameworks** – including access to information laws, conflict-of-interest rules, etc. – to reinforce a culture of integrity in public institutions. Achieving compliance is a particular challenge when governments enter into new fields of policy or regulation, such as lobbying. The Framework therefore also outlines a coherent spectrum of strategies and practices to support implementation and enforcement.

Developing an appropriate framework

Developing a framework for enhancing transparency and accountability in lobbying to maintain trust in government should begin with clarifying public concerns. Careful analysis should take into account available options – including policy measures, voluntary and mandatory regulation – with the aim of drawing up a proposal that adequately addresses public concerns.

To develop a suitable policy response that aims at fostering trust in public decision making while preserving the benefits of the free flow of information to decision makers by lobbyists, it is necessary to **understand properly the essence of the challenge**: why public concern has pushed lobbying to the political agenda. Clarifying the public's concern – whether it is related to accessibility to decision makers, the integrity of government decision making and/or apparent conduct in lobbying – provides decision makers with directions for developing proportional responses to address them:

- When concern is related to **accessibility to decision makers**, measures to provide a level playing field for all stakeholders interested in participating in the development of public policies is indispensable – for instance to ensure that not only the "privileged", but also the "public" has a voice.
- When public concern is about the **integrity of government decision making**, measures to ensure transparency and accountability – for instance through enhanced openness in the decision-making process, lobbyist registration and regular disclosure of lobbying activities – become essential in enabling the public to exercise, in line with freedom of information legislation, the right to know who attempts to influence public decisions.
- If perceived **conduct in lobbying** raises public concern, clear standards of expected conduct should be established – for instance by setting standards of conduct for public officials, in particular decision makers, and by a voluntary or mandatory code for lobbyists.

Better understanding of public concerns also provides policy makers with indications to **determine the most appropriate form of proposed measures** for achieving compliance. For instance, whether compliance with proposed standards could be achieved on a voluntary basis or whether there is a need for legislation or regulation which gives "teeth" through the legal framework.

Standards and rules related to lobbying must respect and conform to the socio-political and administrative context in each jurisdiction. In particular, lobbying regulation should take into account constitutional conventions and established democratic practices.

Globalisation has established similar modes of lobbying practices across a wide number of nations, creating common problems and raising similar issues and expectations in diverse societies. However, **standards, rules or even legislation cannot simply be copied from one jurisdiction to another**, as each political system values the intention of policies and regulations differently and varies legislative provisions and judicial practices accordingly.

Any jurisdiction considering the development of policies or regulations for enhancing transparency in lobbying should not only **review the need for standards or regulation**, but also its precise form in light of international experience and its own constitutional tradition. In addition, the prevailing political culture and traditions should also be considered, particularly in relation to institutionalised consultation processes, such as with representatives of employers and employees in "social partnerships" and public hearings.

Standards and rules related to lobbying should be consistent with the wider regulatory framework that fosters good governance.

Effective policies, standards and rules for enhancing transparency in lobbying can neither be initiated nor reformed in isolation. As part of a complex regulatory framework, it **must affect, and be affected by, other elements of the wider regulatory framework** that sets the standards for good governance. For success, the design must take into account what already exists or may be lacking in other policies and regulatory areas, in particular:

- Standards of expected conduct established by **codes of conduct** for public officials.
- Provisions criminalising **undue influencing** of public decision making, such as influence trafficking, bribery and other corruption offences.
- Constitutional right to **petition government**, exercise freedom of speech and association.
- Processes for regularly **consulting** representatives of employers and employees, for example in the framework of "social partnerships".
- Policies and practices for enhancing **citizen engagement** through public consultation and participation.
- Standards and procedures to ensure **access to government information** related to the decision-making process, for instance by freedom of information legislation.
- Judicial and administrative **review** of decisions.
- Rules on **political parties and election campaign financing**.
- Procedures for **reporting corruption, misconduct and providing protection** for whistleblowers.

The design and adjustment of standards and rules for enhancing transparency in lobbying should be harmonised with those elements of the wider regulatory framework that foster a culture of integrity, transparency, accountability and accessibility in government. These **interdependent and mutually reinforcing elements** of the regulatory and policy framework create an environment that fosters good governance.

Fostering a culture of integrity in public organisations and decision making entails clear standards of conduct for public officials when contacted by lobbyists.

Public authorities are **principally responsible for establishing standards of conduct for public officials** who are the target of lobbying. Principles, rules and procedures should give clear directions to public officials with which they are permitted to engage with lobbyists. Decision makers set an example by their personal conduct in their relationship with lobbyists. Public officials have the responsibility to ensure that their contacts with lobbyists are conducted in accordance with relevant principles, rules and procedures set out by the wider regulatory and policy framework, in particular by the codes for decision makers, civil and public service.

Public officials should conduct their communication with lobbyists in a way that **bears the closest public scrutiny**, in particular:

- **Ensuring impartiality** – By avoiding preferential treatment, for instance by providing balanced opportunities for various interest groups to make representations, and by ensuring that information provided to one interest group is also available to all other interest groups.
- **Providing authorised information** – By, for example, avoiding the leak of "confidential information" that is not available to the public, such as classified government information (*e.g.* on policy intention), planned public procurement initiatives or commercially sensitive material (*e.g.* trade secrets).
- **Enhancing transparency** – In public decision-making processes by disclosing information on communication with lobbyists and information received. This could be achieved by, for example, providing an indicative list of interest representation consulted in the formulation of public decisions and a summary of information received from lobbyist in the legislation process.
- **Avoiding conflict of interest** – By disclosing relevant private interests, such as relationships, business interests, investments, outside employment negotiations or job offers that may create actual, potential or apparent conflict-of-interest situations in the decision-making process. In addition, public officials are expected to take necessary steps to resolve or manage conflict-of-interest situations, for instance by withdrawing themselves from the decision-making process. Accepting gifts and hospitality – in particular when they have more than nominal value or are received repeatedly from the same source – could also be interpreted as a signal of obligation or support.

Maintaining trust in government may require the establishment of specific restrictions for public officials leaving their office, in the form of "cooling-off" periods during which they should not lobby their former organisations.

It is increasingly acknowledged that **former public officials with knowledge and access to other public officials are an asset** in the lobbyists' world. Lobbying government by former public officials – the most highlighted part of the "revolving door" phenomenon – is a growing concern in modern democracies.

These concerns are driving some legislators to establish specific restrictions, such as adequate "cooling-off" periods during which former public officials should not lobby their former organisations. Further restrictions might also forbid using "confidential information" or "switching sides". The prohibition against using "confidential information" remains valid until the information becomes unclassified and is made public.

Clearly define the scope of policy or regulation on lobbying

To provide an effective framework for implementation, the scope of policy or regulation for enhancing transparency in lobbying should be clearly defined, in particular:

- **what actors and activities are covered as lobbyists and lobbying; and**
- **provide proper descriptions of exclusions.**

Clear definitions of who is a lobbyist and what activities are considered lobbying are a precondition for effective application of policies or regulations for enhancing transparency in lobbying if they are to **resolve the mystery of "who is trying to influence whom, how and when"** in public decision making. In defining the scope of lobbying activities, a balance should be reached by effectively taking into account the diversity of entities and individuals that may engage in lobbying activities and the need to provide a level playing field for all stakeholders.

Policies or regulations should **primarily target those who receive compensation for carrying out lobbying activities**, such as consultant lobbyists and in-house lobbyists. Where public concern demands it, lobbying activities should be more broadly and inclusively defined to provide a level playing field for all interest groups intending to influence public decisions. The measures for enhancing transparency in lobbying, however, should take into account the specificities of these interest groups.

Definitions can be refined by specifying that **certain classes of actors or activities are excluded from the policies or regulations**. An example of this is communication that is already on public record, such as formal presentations to legislative committees, public hearings and established consultation mechanisms. Such exclusions may reflect constitutional conventions, the socio-political history of the jurisdiction and the practical realities of conducting business between governments. For instance, representatives of other governments are excluded as they act in their official capacity.

Definitions of lobbyists and lobbying should be robust and unambiguous enough to withstand legal challenges.

Definitions should **not allow space for misreading**, misunderstanding or misinterpretation and should be robust and unambiguous to the greatest extent possible. They should be able to withstand legal and court challenges. Vague and partial definitions of who is covered by the policies or regulations and what activities are encompassed could well endanger the proper functioning of policies or regulations for enhancing transparency in lobbying and lead to non-compliance. Moreover, it can increase public cynicism about the effectiveness of the policy or regulation and jeopardise efforts to maintain public trust.

Establish clear standards and procedures for collecting and disclosing information on lobbying

Disclosure requirements can generate much information. However, an effective lobbying regulation should ensure that:

- **collected information is relevant to the core objectives of ensuring transparency, integrity and efficacy; and**
- **demands for information are realistic in practical and legal terms.**

Disclosure is at the heart of effective regulation for enhancing transparency in lobbying. An effective disclosure system should **provide officials and the public with sufficient information to clearly identify lobbying activities**. When public concern is about decisions being made out of the public eye, key objectives are to:

- establish policy or regulation in order to disclose information on who is trying to influence public decisions; and
- develop supportive transparency measures and mechanisms that enable the public to exercise its right to know.

Examples of the latter might include lobbyist registration and periodical reporting. Moreover, social responsibility considerations may encourage voluntary disclosure by corporations about their participation in public policy development and lobbying.

The public's right to know should be balanced however with **avoiding excessive demand** which, in turn, can create a burdensome disclosure system that may collapse under its own weight, or could encourage non-compliance or delays in providing the information.

In addition, the demand for information should be **carefully balanced with considerations of legitimate exemptions to openness** – for instance to protect confidential information, such as trade secrets, as well as to avoid collusion. Consequently, decision makers should consider how to strike a proper balance. This will ensure that the information requested by disclosure is crucial to achieve the declared objectives of policy or regulation.

Enhanced openness is crucial for maintaining trust in government and public decisions. Therefore, meaningful disclosure should **provide pertinent but parsimonious information** on key aspects of lobbying activities in order to shed light on how public decisions were influenced by stakeholders or vested interests.

Core disclosure requirements should elicit information that:

- **captures the intent of lobbying activity;**
- **identifies its beneficiaries; and**
- **points to those offices and institutions that are its targets.**

Disclosure requirements should, at a minimum, solicit lobbyists to **identify the interest being represented** by naming their clients and beneficiaries, as well as **providing details on the objectives of lobbying activities**. This core information should be disclosed in regular reports in a public registry. Proper identification of clients and actual beneficiaries of lobby activities may well require financial disclosure to recognise main actors in strategic alliances or behind front groups.

Moreover, lobbyists should disclose information on the **government offices** and institutions being lobbied in their regular reports in a public registry.

When contacting public officials, lobbyists may also be required to **identify themselves**, for example, with registration numbers, passes, badges or similar authorisation.

Supplementary disclosure requirements should take into consideration the legitimate information needs of key players in the public decision-making process as well as facilitate public scrutiny.

Even when regulation succeeds in securing core information on lobbying, it will not necessarily satisfy the legitimate information needs of key players in the government decision-making process. Depending on these needs and on any other existing information systems related to a process in which "lobbying" occurs, **supplementary disclosure may be required from lobbyists**, in particular by:

- **Decision makers** – Legislators and ministers may want to know where lobbying pressure comes from to understand whether it reflects broad domestic public opinion or foreign interests. They may also want information about lobbying coalitions and techniques or the fees involved in lobbying in order to understand the power of money for lobbying activities.
- **Citizens** – In order to facilitate public scrutiny, for example through civil society organisations and the media, supplementary disclosure may be required to reveal the relative attention paid to competing groups of interest; spending details, in particular the large expenditures to generate grassroots

communications, lobbying techniques, organisational membership, and, where permitted, arrangements for success fees or "contingency payments". Evolving public expectations may also demand supplementary information, such as clarification of whether the clients and beneficiaries represented had previously received public funding or contracts.

- **Watchdog bodies** – Public offices in charge of detecting, investigating and prosecuting breaches of rules may want records that help them track potentially illicit lobbying undertakings, for example by reviewing financial disclosures. They may need to verify, for example, whether lobbyists were former public officials or may need to be cleared for security purposes (for example checking criminal records). In addition, where prosecution is contemplated, documentation and extensive records are essential; regulation may be best served if lobbyists are required to hold relevant records for a given period, or to file them in a separate process.

However, policy makers and legislators should also bear in mind that requesting too much information can also obscure disclosure on lobbying activities. To **avoid information overload**, when policy makers and legislators consider adding considerably more disclosure requirements to registries, they may find it helpful to establish two-tier registry sites so that core disclosure can be supplemented by more extensive reporting, for instance in sensitive sectors. However, decision makers should also take into consideration that the more complex the disclosure system is, the more expensive and difficult it is to supply and manage it.

Policy makers and legislators may also consider **defining information requirements according to the type of lobbyist**. In case of disclosure of supporters, the category of lobbyists would determine the kind of information required. For instance, on one hand, information about clients and corporate affiliations that fund lobbying would be appropriate supplementary disclosure from consultant lobbyists. On the other hand, requiring information on significant interests involved in their lobbying activities would be more important from not-for-profit organisations.

To adequately serve the public interest, disclosures on lobbying activities should be made in a registry and updated in a timely manner in order to provide credible and up-to-date information to the public and public officials.

Reporting deadlines are as important as disclosure itself to provide timely information on what takes place in the world of lobbying. An effective lobbying disclosure system **requires timely registration and periodic reporting** of lobbying activities to provide credible and up-to-date information that satisfies legitimate demands for effective analysis.

New information and communication technologies, in particular **electronic filing** through the Internet, make possible the collection, processing and dissemination of large quantities of information. Disclosure through electronic filing and reporting provides numerous benefits, in particular:

- **Convenience** – Registrants can file efficiently from their offices.
- **Flexibility** – Forms can elicit quantifiable information for analysis. New information technologies also allow filing of copies of existing documents and reports.
- **Accessibility** – Internet access to reports eliminates the physical centralisation of information and makes that information readily available to members of the public as well as officials, thereby facilitating transparency and public scrutiny.
- **Comparability** – Structured information can facilitate analysis and avoid information overload, for example by using hyperlinks for providing further details on specific aspects of lobbying.
- **Cost-effectiveness** – Information can be easily stored with substantially reduced archival and documentation storage costs.

As members of the public could have difficulty analysing much of the information that can be made available, the **registry processes** should be innovative in developing forms that elicit genuinely useful and reliable information. Registration and reporting forms should properly structure disclosed information in order to avoid overload – as providing too much information can obscure lobbying activities just as effectively as providing too little – as well as facilitate research, control and public scrutiny.

Set standards of conduct to foster a culture of integrity in lobbying

Lobbyists share the responsibility for fostering a culture of integrity in lobbying by setting standards for professionalism, openness and transparency by self-regulation.

While public authorities have the principal task of establishing clear standards of conduct for public officials who are lobbied, lobbyists share the responsibility for avoiding undue influences and ensuring integrity in lobbying since "**it takes two to lobby**". Self-regulation in the form of professional codes, developed by associations of lobbyists or professional bodies, should be encouraged to establish expected standards of conduct for lobbyists themselves.

Professional codes may state ground rules for lobbyists in their relations with public officials, with other lobbyists, with their clients and with the public, for instance to avoid representing conflicting or competing interests. Professional codes play a crucial role in promoting integrity by clarifying expected standards of conduct as well as setting possible sanctions when stated standards are breached. However, without proper measures and resources for implementation and enforcement, self-regulation cannot achieve its desired objectives.

When significant public concern is raised by the conduct of lobbyists, public authorities should consider the establishment of clear conduct requirements of lobbyists in line with public expectations.

When the perceived conduct of lobbyists raises significant public concern, maintaining trust in government decision making would require governments and legislators to set professional and ethical standards of conduct for lobbyists. Standards of conduct for lobbyists could be imposed either by policy, for example, as a condition of access to public officials, or as part of legislation. The goal of such standards of conduct is to **promote principles of good governance**, in particular:

- **Integrity and honesty** – Requiring lobbyists to conduct their relations with public officials with integrity and honesty.
- **Transparency** – Requiring lobbyists to disclose relevant information, such as beneficiaries and the intent of their lobbying activity, when making a representation to public officials. In addition, lobbyists may be required to register and report their lobby activities to the registry in a timely manner.
- **Accuracy of information** – Ensuring the reliability of data provided to public officials, including the means of obtaining information. Lobbyists should use proper care to avoid the dissemination of misleading information.
- **Avoiding conflict of interest** – Requiring lobbyists to avoid conflicts of interest in their representations as well as not to place public officials in conflict-of-interest situations. Moreover, lobbyists should take careful measures when hiring former officials to avoid the breaching of their "cooling-off period" applied for former public officials.

Put in place mechanisms for effective implementation to secure compliance

To enhance compliance, a coherent spectrum of strategies and practices should involve key actors and also carefully balance incentives and sanctions.

Achieving compliance is a particular challenge when governments enter into new policy or regulatory fields, such as lobbying. Setting up unambiguous rules, especially by providing clear definitions for the scope, is a precondition for successfully applying policies and regulations in daily practice.

However, putting regulations into effect also necessitates the **involvement of all key actors**, in particular public officials and lobbyists, to establish a common understanding of expected standards in daily practice. Moreover, ensuring compliance – both voluntary and mandatory – entails the design and application of carefully balanced incentives and sanctions in a coherent spectrum of strategies and practices, in particular, through:

- **Communication** – To raise awareness of expected standards, a vigorous programme of communication is just as vital for securing compliance as stern sanctions. Formal policies and regulations are not effective unless there is a mobilisation of key actors, including lobbyists, public officials and citizens, for instance to clarify public expectations about the policy or regulations for enhancing transparency in lobbying.
- **Education** – To develop proper understanding, commitment and skills for applying the rules and policies in daily practice through providing guidance, for instance in the form of training, advice and focused discussions. Education should not exclusively target public officials but should also reach out to lobbyists and the public, for example, to enable citizens to exercise their right to information related to public decision making and support compliance with the principles, rules and procedures under which public officials are permitted to engage with lobbyists.
- **Formal reporting** – To provide official information by the administering body or independent audit on implementation and functioning of policy or regulation. Such reports could also provide data on the level of compliance, for instance on registrations and filings, detected breaches and applied sanctions, and support interpretation.
- **Leadership** – To create an organisational culture that promotes integrity and openness in daily practice. Senior officials especially set examples through their daily conduct, for instance, when they consistently verify the status of lobbyists, or refuse contact with non-registered lobbyists.
- **Managerial directives** – Such as requiring public officials to verify lobbyists' credentials, keep records of contacts with lobbyists and report possible infractions since officials being lobbied are in the best position to require lobbyists to observe codes of conduct and to report failures to do so. Procedures that necessitate lobbyists to carry passes, badges or similar authorisation in public offices, or require lobbyists to name their clients and beneficiaries when they contact public officials, convey a visible signal about commitment to ensuring compliance. Keeping records of post-public employment restrictions for former public officials (*e.g.* on the required "cooling-off period") also facilitates compliance.
- **Incentives** – A comprehensive strategy carefully balances risks with incentives both for public officials (*e.g.* rewarding compliance of civil servants in their annual performance appraisal) and for lobbyists (*e.g.* providing access to an automatic alert system for consultation and relevant documents,

convenient registration and reporting through electronic filing, making registration a prerequisite to lobbying) to create a culture of compliance with requirements of registration, disclosure and stated standards of conduct.

- **Sanctions** – Combining traditional and new innovative approaches to establish visible and proportional sanctions. Traditional sanctions may range from financial sanctions (*e.g.* fines) through administrative sanctions (*e.g.* cancelling lobbyists from the registry and/or debarring them from the registry for a pre-determined period of time) to criminal prosecution in case of illicit influencing. In addition, more innovative approaches – for example public reporting of confirmed breaches ("naming and shaming") which generates significant media interest – could similarly provide a powerful sanction where reputation is an important asset.
- **Co-ordination** – To ensure the coherence of distinct measures. Each element of a compliance regime should reinforce the others to jointly achieve the overall objectives of policy or regulation, namely enhancing transparency, accountability and integrity in lobbying.

Effective enforcement of lobbying policy or regulation entails not only available dissuasive sanctions but also their timely application in case of a breach of stated standards.

Applying sanctions in case of non-compliance is a vital ingredient of strategies and practices for enforcing policies or regulations for enhancing transparency in lobbying. Visible and proportional sanctions should be applied for both lobbyists and public officials in a timely manner to **provide "teeth" for effective enforcement**.

Effective enforcement also depends on co-operation with officials who are lobbied. Public officials may well assist enforcement by reporting failures to comply with the policy or regulation. Officials also play a critical role in ensuring that lobbyists who have been formally denied access, for instance lobbyists cancelled from the registry, are not allowed to circumvent such exclusion. Procedures should also facilitate citizens' **reporting of breaches** to comply with rules for enhancing transparency in lobbying.

Administrators of policy or regulation for enhancing transparency in lobbying should be independent of political pressure and provided with sufficient resources to effectively carry out their responsibilities.

Although possible sanctions are a necessary feature of any policy or regulation, they are rarely sufficient on their own to constitute a strong deterrent.

Adequate institutional arrangements are also indispensable for administering policies or regulations for enhancing transparency in lobbying, in particular:

- **Status** – Ensuring administrative independence of officials from political pressure. For instance, appointing the principal officials responsible for implementing policy or enforcing regulations for a pre-determined period and clearly defining the conditions for their removal.
- **Capacity** – Administering offices should be provided with the resources necessary to effectively implement policies or regulations (*e.g.* through communication and education) and monitor compliance (*e.g.* to detect breaches).

Securing the objectives of lobbying policies or regulations may also require that officials have the authority to provide interpretation, to review filings, to demand clarifications from registrants, on the one hand, and to pursue investigations further, if necessary, to the point of notifying the need for criminal enquiries, on the other hand.

Effective enforcement requires that officials in charge of administering policy or regulation are provided with **operational competence** necessary to ensure compliance. This includes, for instance:

- **Authority** – To provide interpretation for supporting daily application, to review and verify timeliness and accuracy of disclosed information in order to detect non-compliance and to take timely action, such as requiring further information or rectification of disclosure refusing and revoking registration when requirements are not met. Moreover, to carry out investigation of alleged breaches may require specific authority.
- **Sufficient timeframe** – To identify infractions and carry out investigations of complaints of alleged breaches.
- **Clear actions** – To be taken in case of non-compliance that may range from informal warning, formal warning, order for corrective action, to referral for investigation and criminal prosecution.
- **Taking timely and proper measures** – To send a signal of visible commitment in order to ensure enforcement.

The public has a right to know how public decisions were influenced by stakeholders and interests. When there is so much at stake that competition for public goods may make it impossible to achieve compliance with lobbying policies or regulations on a voluntary basis, mandatory regulations and codes may be needed to achieve the principles of transparency, accountability and integrity in lobbying.

Principles of transparency, accountability and integrity cannot be adopted half-heartedly. In order to ensure a level playing field for all stakeholders interested in influencing government decision making, **policy or regulation for enhancing transparency in lobbying should be accepted and applied by all actors** in lobbying. When compliance with policy or regulation for enhancing transparency in lobbying cannot be achieved on a voluntary basis, increased public concern may persuade governments to explore mandatory regulation.

Successful compliance largely depends on the **level of enforcement** that can be achieved at the governmental level. Public authorities can:

- Require public officials to report the failure of lobbyists to comply with regulations.
- Investigate failures and prosecute breaches of regulations.
- Impose a variety of sanctions such as the denial of access to public officials.
- Require lobbyists to disclose information.

In order to meet the growing expectations of society for good governance, governments should review the functioning of lobbying policies or regulations on a regular basis and make necessary adjustments in light of experience with implementation.

Policies and regulations for enhancing transparency in lobbying are often developed incrementally as part of the political and administrative learning process. Putting policies and regulations into effect and regularly reviewing their implementation and impact allows policy makers to better **understand what factors influence compliance** with stated standards, rules and procedures.

The **refinement** of specific policies and regulations for enhancing transparency in lobbying should be seen as only part of a process of enhancing the integrated and interdependent body of policies and regulations to meet public expectations for effectively implementing the principles of transparency, accountability and integrity in lobbying.

Notes

1. Statement of Chairman Alexander Pechtold, Minister of Government Reform and Kingdom Relations, the Netherlands, 28 November 2005 in Rotterdam. The full text of the Statement can be consulted at *www.oecd.org/dataoecd/0/11/35806296.pdf*. Further information on the event is available at *www.modernisinggovernment.com/*.
2. The Compact Edition of the *Oxford English Dictionary* notes that the noun "lobby" has quite old roots going back to the 17th century: "In the House of Commons, and other houses of legislature, a large entrance-hall or apartment open to the public, and chiefly serving for interviews between members and persons not belonging to the House."
3. According to the *Green Paper of the European Transparency Initiative* "lobbying means all activities carried out with the objective of influencing the policy formulation and decision-making processes of the European institutions". The Green Paper defines

lobbyists "as persons carrying out such activities, working in a variety of organisations such as public affairs consultancies, law firms, NGOs, think-tanks, corporate lobby units ('in-house representatives') or trade associations".

4. For example, the Global Reporting Initiative (GRI) requires disclosure on lobbying and participation in public policy development, as well as the total value of financial and in-kind contributions to political parties, politicians and related institutions. For further information, consult the GRI Reporting Framework at *www.globalreporting.org/ReportingFrameworkDownloads/*.

5. The Special Session on Lobbying: Enhancing Transparency and Accountability brought together policy makers and leading experts on 7-8 June 2007 in Paris. Further details, including agenda, documents and presentation slides can be consulted at *www.oecd.org/gov/ethics*.

6. The European Commission launched the European Transparency Initiative in November 2005. The Green Paper addresses the need for a more structured framework for the activities of interest representatives/lobbyists. Follow-up to the Green Paper can be viewed at *http://ec.europa.eu/transparency/eti/results_en.htm*.

7. The Recommendation and Guiding Principles can be consulted at *www.oecd.org/document/38/0,3343,en_2649_34141_2753254_1_1_1_1,00.html*.

Bibliography

European Commission (2006), "Green Paper of the European Transparency Initiative", COM(2006) 194 final, *http://ec.europa.eu/transparency/eti/docs/gp_en.pdf*.

European Commission (2008), "Code of Conduct for Interest Representatives", *https://webgate.ec.europa.eu/transparency/regrin/infos/codeofconduct.do?locale=en#en*.

OECD (1995), "OECD Recommendation on Improving the Quality of Government Regulation", Public Governance and Territorial Development Directorate, OECD, Paris.

OECD (1998), "OECD Recommendation on Improving Ethical Conduct in the Public Service". Public Governance and Territorial Development Directorate, OECD, Paris.

OECD (2003), "OECD Recommendation on Guidelines for Managing Conflict of Interest in the Public Service", Public Governance and Territorial Development Directorate, OECD, Paris, *www.oecd.org/dataoecd/17/23/33967052.pdf*.

OECD (2006a), "Lobbying: Key Policy Issues", internal working document, Public Governance and Territorial Development Directorate, OECD, Paris.

OECD (2006b), "Governance Arrangements to Ensure Transparency in Lobbying: A Comparative Overview", internal working document, Public Governance and Territorial Development Directorate, OECD, Paris.

OECD (2009), "Self-Regulation and Regulation of the Lobbying Profession", OECD Global Forum on Public Governance, 4-5 May 2009, OECD, Paris.

Lobbyists, Governments and Public Trust, Volume 1
Increasing Transparency through Legislation

Chapter 2

Comparative Review of Legislation for Enhancing Transparency and Accountability in Lobbying[1]

Globalisation has established similar modes of lobbying practices across a wide number of nations, creating common problems and raising similar issues and expectations in diverse societies. This chapter provides a comparative overview of trends, approaches, models and examples of country solutions considered to be "state of the art" and that take into account the social and political context in North America, Europe and Australia.

The comparative overview is structured around the following set of questions that might logically guide the framing of standards and rules for enhancing transparency and accountability in lobbying:

- *First, concerning the issue of definition, who is to be regulated? This is a fundamentally difficult issue for some countries and in some situations.*
- *Second, what should be required to be disclosed and how? Disclosure is the heart of lobby regulation, and the most difficult to formulate parsimoniously.*
- *Codes of conduct, in various forms, are addressed by asking how lobbyists can be regulated, and led on to the issue of securing compliance.*
- *Finally, how can the integrity of lobby regulation be ensured?*

Summary

This chapter looks at existing rules, legislation and academic literature to provide a comparative overview of trends, approaches and models with selected examples of country solutions. This comparative overview supports the identification of building blocks and emerging principles, presented in the previous chapter, to provide decision makers with guidance for enhancing transparency and accountability in lobbying. This chapter reviews in particular the country contexts which affect lobbying legislation regulation, and fundamental administrative principles.

Interest in lobby regulation reflects the **globalisation of lobby practices**, which have disrupted long-standing systems of relations between government and interests in OECD countries and beyond. While a trend appears, at least in North America and Europe, toward heightened lobby regulation, that trend has two opposing aspects. Globalisation has diffused modes of lobbying across nations, creating common problems and raising similar issues in diverse societies. But, at the same time, each political system values the objectives of regulation differently and varies legislative provisions accordingly.

Consequently, it is not wise to propose regulations that can be copied from one jurisdiction to another. Indeed, an attempt to identify building blocks for a framework should not be confused with the creation of regulation that can be applied uniformly across jurisdictions. The best that one can hope to do is to **identify a number of common situations that may be addressed in similar, but not identical, ways**. This caveat is particularly pertinent in Europe, where nations with corporatist traditions are experiencing the tension between two forces: *i)* globalisation; and *ii)* respect for "social partnerships" that have served them well for many decades. It follows that each legislature has to review both the need for regulation and its precise form in the light not only of international experience, but of its own constitutional arrangements and its prevailing political culture.

Having identified broad contextual influences on lobby regulation, this chapter **examines what is considered to be "state of the art" in the field**, bearing in mind a series of questions that might logically guide the framing of standards and rules for enhancing transparency and accountability in lobbying. To identify the target, the following questions can be asked:

- First, **who is to be regulated?** This is a fundamentally difficult issue for some countries and in some situations.

- Second, **what should they be required to disclose?** This is the meat of lobby regulation, and the most difficult to formulate parsimoniously.
- Codes of conduct, in various forms, are addressed by asking **how lobbyists can be regulated**, and led on to the issue of securing compliance.
- Finally, points were made in response to the question: **How can the integrity of lobby regulation be ensured?**

Lobby regulations have developed incrementally as part of the process of political learning. Exercises in lobby regulation have ranged from registering interests appearing before legislative committees to requiring extensive disclosure of lobby undertakings. Regulatory schemes vary, depending on the cultural and constitutional background of each state. These variations make it impractical to recommend a uniform pattern of regulation at this time.

Nevertheless, the globalisation of lobby practices and governments' endorsement of the **principles of transparency and integrity** are leading states to register lobbyists and to begin to formulate standards of disclosure. To date, these standards of disclosure elicit information that:

- captures the intent of lobbying activity;
- identifies its beneficiaries; and
- points to those offices and institutions that are its targets.

Electronic filing has revolutionised lobby regulation, making it possible to collect and disseminate large quantities of information. But, there are limits to its application. Both compliance and timely and effective analysis are enhanced if disclosures are pertinent, but parsimonious. Conversely, some information needs – such as criminal prosecution – demand documentation and extensive records. For such purposes, regulation may be best served if lobbyists are required to hold records for a given period, or must file them in a separate process.

Where transparency and integrity are the principal goals of regulation, effectiveness is best achieved if definitions are broad and inclusive, and the theatre of lobby activity is also defined broadly and inclusively, while **compliance is best secured** if definitions, and exemptions, are:

- unambiguous and clearly understood by lobbyists and office holders;
- practical in application; and
- robust enough to support legal challenges.

Furthermore, registry officials need the authority to require additional information and to carry out investigations. To secure compliance, however, extensive education programmes, can be as important as enforcing the rules with powerful sanctions.

Regulation of lobbyists' behaviour has focused on codes of conduct. These establish principles of behaviour – such as honesty, openness and professionalism – and rules to enforce them. **Currently, debate centres on whether codes should be voluntary or imposed by law; experience suggests that legislative regulation is preferable.** In considering the impact of codes, and other regulatory features of lobbying legislation, it should be remembered that lobby regulation cannot be free-standing. It is part of a regulatory regime consisting of laws, policies and practices that are interdependent and establish the principles of good governance across the public sector.

Finally, securing and maintaining the integrity of the regulations requires that officials have sufficient resources, powers and independence to enable them to carry out their functions.

State of the art: Current models for regulating lobbying

The globalisation of lobby regulation

Lobbying is a necessary adjunct to modern government. Complex regulations, labyrinthine bureaucracies, lengthy and diffused decision processes baffle individual citizens and tax the resources of most businesses. Few can afford to pursue their interests independently of experienced and informed advisors. Acting as guides, intermediaries and interlocutors, these advisors have become indispensable.

Lobbying has not only become a reality, its legitimacy is widely recognised. In democracies, citizens have the right to petition government and it is legitimate for them to pay third parties in order to do so. However, just as the complexity of modern government necessitates lobbying, so the proliferation of lobbying activity introduces many new actors into policy processes, so that those processes become obscured and an environment is created where coercion and corruption can occur. Thus, the regulation of lobbying becomes necessary.

The purpose of this chapter is to identify, through examination of existing rules, legislation and academic literature, **a set of building blocks and principles** that might provide a framework for enhancing transparency and accountability in lobbying. It will first consider the contexts which affect regulation and then turn to the more complex issues of regulation. The chapter will address broad themes, rather than the detailed provisions which frequently reflect idiosyncratic events. For example, the definition of who is a lobbyist, or what is lobbying, is clearly an important issue wherever regulation has been considered, but the exclusion of provincial or state officials is a provision that applies to federal systems. In addition to discussing the legislative provisions for monitoring and regulation, this chapter will look at some fundamental administrative principles.

Convergence and disparity in the regulatory environment

For over a century, the **United States was the sole jurisdiction to regulate lobbyists**, though many countries had legislated against bribery and other means of influencing government officials. In 1991, a Library of Congress Survey found that only three other countries, Australia, Canada, and Germany had instituted lobbyist legislation (Clarke, 1991). In 2004, a similar survey, conducted by Margaret Mary Malone of the Irish Institute of Public Administration reported that "countries with specific rules and regulations governing the activities of lobbyists and interest groups are more the exception than the rule" (Malone, 2004). Even these, with the demise in 1995 of the Australian registry, had declined in number. Nevertheless, Malone concluded that:

> In states where informal practices and conventions continue to prevail, the issue of more formal regulation of lobbyists is advancing up the political agenda. Typically, political scandals highlight undue influence on the part of certain interest groups *vis-à-vis* decision makers in the public domain. There is, consequently, greater public and political pressure for more formal regulation. Nor is there necessarily resistance to this pressure. There is evidence to suggest that some lobbyists would welcome greater regulation in order to set themselves apart from those who threaten to bring the profession into disrepute.
>
> Throwing public light on the relationship between civil society and government (politicians and bureaucrats) is increasingly regarded as a desirable and necessary development in the interests of good government (Malone, 2004).

This convergence is deceptive. Examination of the legislation adopted by different countries reveals **a variety of reasons for and understandings about lobby regulation**, even though the same terms – transparency, integrity, and, to a lesser extent, efficacy – inform the language of legislation and its supporting rhetoric. Broadly speaking regulation does address transparency, integrity and efficacy, but national perceptions of each differ, and their regulations display quite different approaches to attaining them. These variations are systemic, reflecting constitutional arrangements and political cultures rooted in disparate national experience. To illustrate: in European and North American countries public philosophies deem it illegal for a public servant to seek or receive "anything of value personally for or because of any official act performed or to be performed" (Samuels, 2006). Where Confucian philosophy has influenced political culture, however, gift-giving has long been an accepted part of the relationship between citizens and officials, a tradition that attenuates the impact of anti-bribery laws (Hrebenar *et al.*, 1998; Grant Jordan, 1998). On another level, corporatist systems in Europe encourage organisational integration in policy-making processes. Sector associations participate, virtually by right, in consultative bodies. A body of law and convention has evolved over the last century to regulate their participation. In those systems, lawmakers have demonstrated uncertainty about the appropriate methods for regulating newcomers, such as consultant lobbyists and public interest groups with broad international memberships, to their policy systems (Ronit and Schneider, 1998). North American systems, on the other hand, first applied registration and regulation to consultant lobbyists, but have not been as successful as the European's in integrating associations in policy processes [Thomas (ed.), 2004].

Polish example

Several strands of development are at work here. The **global diffusion of democratic concepts and practices through the media and international interest groups** may be persuasive, but not easily adapted to the practices, understandings and governmental arrangements that prevail in individual countries. These may be undergoing radical change. Adoption effectively means adaptation. Poland's recent legislation illustrates this point. The first words of the Act on legislative and regulatory lobbying would be familiar to any North American lobbyist or official:

> This Act lays down the rules of openness governing legislative and regulatory lobbying and the rules governing professional lobbying, determines the forms in which control can be exercised over professional lobbying, and sets out the rules for the keeping of the Register of Professional Lobbyists and Lobbying Firms[2] (Act of 7 July 2005 on legislative and regulatory lobbying, Article 1).

However, as the "rules of openness governing legislative lobbying" are enunciated, it is evident that the act has quite a different purpose from its counterparts in the United States and Canada. Rather than setting out a regime for disclosing contacts between officials and lobbyists and the methods used to influence decisions, the Polish act **establishes a procedure whereby government declares its legislative intentions** (Act of 7 July 2005, Chapter 2, Article 3.1) and initiates procedures that allow interested parties to register their concerns and proposals for change *vis-à-vis* specific legislative and regulatory projects and to announce their intention to participate in public discussions of those proposals. Admission to these discussions is contingent on registration. In other words, while the Polish act does establish a register of lobbyists, its principal sections are more concerned with creating procedures for public consultation than with providing the type of lobby regulation familiar in North America.

The significance of the **differences in policy processes between European and North American systems** becomes apparent as one considers questions of definition. The free-wheeling environment of policy making in the United States, and to a lesser extent Canada, fosters an industry where entry is virtually uncontrolled; and both consultant and in-house lobbyists can, as long as they are adequately supported financially, exploit access to a variety of decision points. Lobbyists thrive as nimble and versatile guides to complex, diffuse and dynamic systems. On the other side of the coin, from the perspective of the general public and often of government itself, that very flexibility is a source of concern. It obscures policy processes and confuses issues. Hence, the flexibility calls for transparency, and attempts to bring some order to the lobbying scene by forcing lobbyists to disclose details of their undertakings. Because those undertakings, in one form or another, involve an element of compensation, North American legislators have felt that it is entirely logical that this process of regulation should begin by defining lobbyists in terms of their financial relationship to clients or employers.

Box 2.1. **Corporatist systems and lobbying**

In corporatist systems a degree of order already exists. Historically, the approach to policy making has been more structured, particularly in economic realms. **Formal industry and labour associations have had a recognised place** in the deliberations that lead to government policy. It was not necessary to require them to register as lobbyists, because their participation was already known, the processes were defined, and the interests of the associations were familiar to the public as well as officials. Malone's description of Austrian practice illustrates these processes:

> Large economic interest groups such as employers' organisations and trade unions do have a significant input into the making of law in the context of the "social partnership". When preparing a bill, the government must consult with the chambers or *Kammern*, which are statutory representatives of interest groups, under the "appraisal procedure". In general, the government consults not only the chambers but other interest groups also. At the parliamentary stage, the social partners exert influence through personal and political contacts. In the past, such informal contacts were greatly facilitated by the fact that more than 50% of MPs had close ties or were members of interest groups such as employers' associations or trade unions. This is no longer the case (Clarke, 1991).

Globalisation has brought **two quite different challenges** to these understandings in corporatist systems. In economic sectors, the rise of multinational corporations has meant that foreign concerns have sought entry not only to national markets, but also to the decision-making processes that influence those markets. Inevitably local economic interests resisted entry at both levels, prompting intruder corporations to turn to lobbying firms that could offer both local knowledge and familiarity with North American lobbying techniques. International social movement groups have presented a somewhat different challenge to corporatist systems. They have encouraged public expectations for participation in social policy making, whilst raising issues that corporatist structures were not well organised to process.

Box 2.1. **Corporatist systems and lobbying** *(cont.)*

The effect on corporatist systems has been to create **two additional pressure patterns** in policy systems. In the economic sphere, consultant lobbying competes with the traditional weight of associations in policy deliberations, while in the fields of social policy, the pressures from social movement groups are more public and overtly political. These new tensions, and new complexities, have contributed to a growing interest in adopting – but also adapting – North American-style lobby regulation in corporatist countries.

The lesson to be learned from this is that it cannot be assumed that all lobby regulation is based on identical understandings of public need, or even that clauses that appear to be comparable across jurisdictions do in fact have the same purpose or the same effect. Hence, review of lobbying legislation in different jurisdictions recognises that each political system values the objectives of regulation differently and varies legislative provisions accordingly. In addition to appreciating these cultural forces, it must be kept in mind that it is also fundamental that lobby regulation conform to the constitutional conventions of specific countries.[1]

1. For a useful discussion of the constitutional underpinnings of the Quebec Lobbying, Transparency and Ethics Act see Henri Brun and Guy Tremblay "The public's right to know who is trying to influence the government: A fundamental right" (*"Le droit du public de savoir qui cherche à influencer le gouvernement : un droit fondamental"*), *Éthique publique*, 8 (2006) 1, pp. 123-136.

Right to petition

In Canada and the United States, for example, **bills of rights set limits to lobby regulation**. Care must be taken to distinguish the exercise of constitutional rights from the lobbying functions. Individuals seeking any kind of government benefit for themselves are generally within their rights when they seek meetings with officials and present arguments supporting their case. These individuals are certainly lobbying, but because they are exercising the right to petition on their own behalf, are not "lobbyists" as defined by most regulations. Similarly, volunteers who lobby to promote a cause also are exercising the right to petition, to associate with others of the same persuasion, and to exercise the freedom to speak in support of the cause.

It follows that regulation, to be effective, must respect the political culture and governmental system of the society in which it operates. It also follows that the attempt to identify principles for regulation should not be confused with the creation of legislation that can be applied uniformly across jurisdictions. Each legislature has to review both the need for regulation and its precise form in the light not only of international experience, but of its own constitutional arrangements and its prevailing political culture.

Italian debate

Italy, for example, has on two occasions considered introducing legislation regulating "public relations activities", but so far debate has foundered on **problems of definition and the nature of the reforms** that are needed. M.C. Allen, in a working document prepared for the European Parliament, quotes the Research Department of the Italian *Camera dei Deputati* (Chamber of Deputies) to the effect that:

> It is generally felt... that there is a need for regulation, accompanied by institutional reform which would change the relationship between interest groups and political groups... It is argued that information should be credible and should therefore be subject to rules of professional conduct. This could be achieved by compiling registers of pressure groups and making it compulsory for registered groups to submit reports stating the expenses incurred and action taken. This would not only improve the quality of information but would provide greater transparency of interest group activities. The introduction of registers would mean deciding on a precise definition of what constitutes "public relations activities" which, in any case, should cover a number of activities which would otherwise not be covered under the law (Crespo Allen, 1996).

To date it appears that only two **local governments**, the Regional Councils of Tuscany and Molise, have adopted lobby regulation in Italy (Government of Tuscany, Italy, 2002). However, in October 2007 the Italian government approved a legislative proposal on lobbying and submitted it to the Parliament for discussion. Lobbying between interest groups and government officials, not including legislators, would be regulated through the National Council for Economics and Labour (CNEL) which would develop a compulsory code of conduct for lobbying activity. Lobbyists would be required to submit annual reports on their activities which, in turn, would be consolidated in the CNEL's annual report on lobbying. In addition, lobbyists would be required to register themselves and the interest they represent. Transparency would be promoted through the provision of access to documents related to lobbying and in the preamble to legislative proposals where officials would be required to declare whether lobbying activity had taken place. Although the Italian government fell in January 2008, the fact that opposition parties supported the proposals suggests that it may remain on the agenda of the newly elected Parliament.

French approach

France, too, in moving toward the adoption of lobby regulation takes an **approach that reflects its own national experience**. The National Assembly in January 2008 acted on a motion submitted by Deputies Patrick Beaudouin and Arlette Grosskost calling for a registry of lobbyists and a code of conduct for lobbyists which would be under the supervision of the Assembly Questors who would have the authority to issue and to remove lobbying permits. The Assembly authorised Deputies Beaudouin and Grosskost to conduct public hearings into the proposal (*Assemblée Nationale*, 2008).

The Bureau of the National Assembly[3] adopted the "rules of transparency and ethics for interest representatives" (*Assemblée Nationale*, 2009) on 2 July 2009. According to these rules, come into effect in October 2009, interest representatives recognised by the Bureau and added to an official list, benefit from badges valid for one day giving them access to the building of the National Assembly and other specific rights. In order to benefit from these rights, interests representatives will have to disclose information related to their activities and the interests they represent for the register[4] and comply with a specific code of conduct[5] for their profession. In case of misconduct the Bureau can withdraw them from the list either temporarily or permanently.

While lobby regulation must accommodate national and local variation, it must also recognise that **globalisation has influenced government policy processes in similar ways around the world**. A number of lobbying firms are themselves multinational organisations. Numerous interest groups are either international in structure, or co-operate through international coalitions. Many nationally-based non-governmental organisations operate globally. Although they generally conform to the practices of host governments, their lobbying techniques inevitably reflect the values and assumptions of their own political systems. Thus, modes of lobbying have been transferred across nations, bringing with them common problems and raising similar issues in diverse societies. The effects are difficult to characterise and really require extensive research. It might be possible in some settings to describe modes of interaction between interests and government in terms of parallel systems; a corporatist track used by domestic interests and a lobby track used by multinational interests, with some larger enterprises engaged at both levels. Elsewhere, there may be a confusing intrusion of newcomers into established patterns of representation. Lawmakers face a considerable challenge as they address the issues raised by the arrival of new actors and new patterns of behaviour while at the same time preserving traditional processes of local representation.

Transparency, integrity and efficacy

Examination of the history of campaigns to introduce existing legislation suggests that transparency, integrity and efficacy are the principal factors driving the adoption of regulation and its main objectives, though, as already stressed, national and regional variations will occur.

Transparency promises to expose to public view the processes that are at work as government decisions are made. It is often promoted as enabling the public to know who is lobbying for what, in order to allow it to take suitable precautions to protect its interest. Transparency is also a means of reassuring the public that officials are working honestly and in the best interests of the community, and an incentive to those who seek public benefits to abide by prevailing norms of honesty (Herrmann, 2006). Transparency sometimes precedes more extensive regulation (Congressional Research Service, 1986).[6]

Transparency and **integrity** are closely related. In a democracy, respect for governmental institutions depends in large part on citizens' confidence that the government is indeed their government, and is not the private preserve of those who can afford to pay for access. Consequently, there must be, amongst policy makers, a general concern to promote equal access to government, exemplary ethical standards in public life, and resistance to the exercise of undue influence.

Since they affect the political classes in general, such concerns cannot be addressed solely by regulation which specifically targets lobbyists. In fact, traditionally, attempts to ensure the integrity of governmental decision making have targeted the officials who actually make those decisions (Hrebenar *et al.*, 1998; Jordan, 1998). Bribery and other forms of corruption were the first objects of regulation. However, as democratic government evolved financial controls were introduced; ethics issues were addressed; election finance became more strictly regulated, and, most recently, transparency in decision making has become a major objective, fostering access-to-information laws, whistleblower legislation and lobbyist regulation. Ultimately a cluster of statutes, conventions and codes, taken together, constitute a regulatory regime that attempts to encompass governmental decision making.

Our concern here is with legislation that specifically addresses the regulation of those who lobby officials. It can be assumed that lobby regulation occurs as one of the more recent accretions of the ethics regime that has evolved in most countries and that laws targeting lobbyists are part of that more extensive regulatory regime,[7] in addition to regulations that seek to govern officials as they interact with lobbyists. Since it is not always easy to distinguish between those who make governmental decisions and those who lobby for those decisions, it must be noted that in some instances public officials, legislators in particular, have to be regulated as lobbyists (Jordan, 1998; Ronit and Schneider, 1998).[8]

Codes of conduct

When looking at legislation that regulates lobbyists, provisions can be found that are directed at promoting integrity including those, such as disclosure rules, which illuminate activity. The most important recent moves toward securing integrity, however, have been the adoption of codes of conduct. Closely related to the ethics packages which have been adopted to regulate the behaviour of officials, **these codes have been attached to registration statutes** and their enforcement made the responsibility of registrars. Although their phrasing is broad, they do provide registry officials with some authority, albeit limited, to monitor compliance with the Act and to investigate lobbying behaviour and, through reports filed with the legislature, to draw public attention to breaches of the code. Taking this approach one step further, Canada has recently enacted legislation which connects the lobbyist registration requirements to regulations that govern the behaviour, including their post-employment behaviour, of senior officials.[9] In the final analysis, however, efforts to ensure integrity depend chiefly on clauses directed at securing compliance.

Efficiency and effectiveness

Lobby regulation is also affected by considerations of efficiency and effectiveness. Since communication is the essence of policy making, lobby regulation cannot be allowed to impede the flow of information from the public, and other official bodies, to lawmakers and their advisors. Consequently, legislators have been reluctant to define lobbying, and lobbying activities, so rigorously that informed members of the public hesitate to offer their views to government, and they generally take pains to exclude officials of other levels of government from the purview of the regulations.[10] **For the general public, efficacy is a less obvious objective** than are transparency and integrity, but for officials and party leaders it is a prominent concern, for they are themselves frequently overwhelmed by the variety and complexity of information showered on them by lobbyists. Laws like those of Germany and Poland can help policy makers by regulating the flow of information to them, while the disclosure rules common in North America facilitate officials' understanding of the sources of policy campaigns, and assist them to evaluate the pressures put upon them to take decisions. Although this information may not show them where the public interest lies, as decisions are made it can guide them away from options contrived and promoted to particularly favour special interests (Greenwood, 2004; Pross, 1991).[11]

The efficacy of lobbying legislation itself is also an important concern. Early regulations were bedevilled by **unrealistic disclosure requirements which undermined the legitimacy of the legislation**. In recent years new information technologies have facilitated registration, permitting refinements in reporting requirements and greatly extending the capacity of both officials and the public to monitor the activities of lobbyists. With improved facilities to actually carry out their assignments, registry officials have sought, and sometimes obtained, the powers needed to carry out investigations and to see that violations are prosecuted. The most recent developments have seen some registrars given a degree of administrative autonomy of the government of the day.

Finally, as a general principle, it is essential that lobby regulation be perceived by all concerned to **serve a useful function**. Perhaps this is the most important lesson to be learned from the Australian experience. There a lobbyist register was instituted in 1983, but abandoned in 1996 because, in the view of the government, it was "toothless and unenforceable", and in the view of others because its provisions were ignored and access to the registered information was highly restricted; in other words, because it failed to serve a useful purpose (Warhurst, 1998).[12]

In conclusion, experience to date suggests that the decision to regulate lobbyists and to introduce regulations that are effective is contingent upon the following underlying factors:

- Lobby regulation is perceived to address broadly accepted public policy objectives, such as: *i)* promoting transparency in governmental decision making; *ii)* supporting integrity in the policy process; and *iii)* enhancing the efficacy of policy processes.
- Regulation is compatible with the constitutional framework and political culture of the adopting jurisdiction.
- Regulation of lobbyists is conceived of as part of a body of regulation – a regime – that governs the ethical behaviour of public officials and those they deal with.
- The viability of the regulations depends on instituting rules of disclosure that can be realistically applied and on ensuring that officials have the powers and administrative autonomy sufficient to enable them to carry out their duties.

The sections that follow will **identify core issues** in lobby regulation while recognising that specific countries will respond differently to them. The challenge is to set out a series of principles that might be considered as a point of reference for decision makers developing a body of lobby regulation. This chapter first identifies the principal features of lobby regulation as it currently exists. It then explores those features from the perspective of a series of questions that should define the regulatory arena.

Box 2.2. **State of the art: Reviewing current models for regulating lobbying**

Though only a few nations have enacted legislation to regulate lobbying, their experience and that of sub-national levels of government enable us to address the key question: what are the elements of strong lobby regulation? The answer to this overarching question is best considered by asking a series of subsidiary questions:

- Who is to be regulated?
- What should they be required to disclose?
- How can they be regulated?
- How can compliance be obtained?
- How can the integrity of lobby regulation be ensured?

Effective regulation will depend on the presence of the following elements:

- There is a clear, unambiguous definition of the regulatory target.
- Disclosure requirements are meaningful and attainable.
- Procedures for securing compliance are effective and realistic.
- The integrity of the regulatory process is maintained by an appropriate administrative framework.

Since the purpose is to identify "a set of principles that might provide a framework for enhancing transparency and accountability insofar as lobbying is concerned", these four elements and the questions which led us to them can be used to organise a discussion of existing measures and proposals for measures. This chapter looks first at issues of definition, then at the complexities of disclosure, the problems of securing compliance, and finally the steps that must be taken to secure the integrity of the regulatory process.

Issues of definition: Who is to be regulated?

Introduction

Clarity is essential to effective lobby regulation. The early history of registration in Australia, Canada and the United States shows that **where lobbyists are not clearly identified and demonstrably required to register, they will not do so**. Equally, where disclosure requirements are not clearly laid out and unambiguously required, they will be ignored.[13]

The following paragraphs discuss some of the more significant issues that have arisen regarding definition. They conclude with an attempt to provide some general observations to assist in dealing with this critically important aspect of regulation.

Leading issues related to definition

As already noted, two classes of policy actors are targeted by regulations governing lobbying. The first are **government officials**, including legislators, who are themselves lobbied; the second are **lobbyists**. Since the former are usually explicitly identified in both lobbying legislation and in the body of regulations that apply to their conduct, it is not necessary to discuss their identification here. The definition of lobbyists, and lobbying activity, being much more troublesome, warrants examination.

Categories of lobbyists

In North America, the obvious targets of lobbyist registration schemes are the fabled "**guns for hire**" of fiction and investigative journalism, or, in the language of much legislation, "consultant lobbyists". That this stereotype is simplistic soon came to be realised, and legislators extended registration to two breeds of "in-house" lobbyists: full-time employees of corporations who were engaged in "government relations" on behalf of their firms, and comparable employees of interest groups. This approach defines a lobbyist as a person who receives some form of remuneration for representing the interests of a third party to government officials. Thus, US Public Law 104-65 (The Lobbying Disclosure Act of 1995, 109 Stat. 691) and the Canadian Lobbyists Registration Act use compensation as the trigger for registration.[14] In Ottawa, a consultant lobbyist is an individual who "for payment, on behalf of any person or organisation" undertakes to communicate with public office holders concerning a specified set of public decisions or to arrange meetings with public office holders. Likewise, an in-house lobbyist is an employee whose duties include communicating with public office holders on behalf of the employer.

Recognising that **consultant and in-house lobbyists** are the front-line actors in the lobbying business has not simplified the task of defining who should be regulated. In fact, defining "lobbying" and determining who is a "lobbyist" has proven particularly difficult in corporatist systems. Earlier this chapter described how the intrusion of multinational corporations and international social movements have challenged corporatist policy-making systems, and encouraged authorities in those system to consider adopting North American-style lobby regulation. Such a project, however, must deal with the challenge of adapting regulatory frameworks that assume no prior privileged position for any group to one that has for decades incorporated certain groups into policy deliberations. Justin Greenwood (2004) reports that for reform-minded members of the European Parliament, "a major obstacle in getting [regulatory] legislation to a vote was the failure to provide a working definition of what constituted a lobbyist". The concept of lobbying was at odds with practice in a number of European states where corporatist structures made legitimate the participation of numerous groups in governmental decision-making processes. How, for example, could the representative of a trade organisation be characterised as a "lobbyist" when he or she was participating, by invitation or by time-honoured tradition, in official advisory committees?

Box 2.3. **Self-definition of lobbyists: Examples of the European Parliament and the United States**

The European Parliament circumvented this problem by providing a set of conditions which, if met, would lead a consultant or organisation employee to register as a lobbyist. Greenwood states:

> ... the regulatory approach proposed by Ford (MEP, Glynn) was politically masterful in that it did not attempt to define a lobbyist, but relied upon self-definition through the incentive of applying for a pass. All those lobbyists wishing to visit the Parliament would find it much easier to obtain a regular pass, available in return for signing a code of conduct, than to stand in line for a day pass (Greenwood, 2004).

Self-definition may have resolved this particular impasse, but it is inherently flawed. It captures only those lobbyists who actually work within the purviews of the European Parliament. Perhaps this is satisfactory, as far as the members of the Parliament are concerned. A similar level of coverage has, until recently, been the norm in the United States. But in other jurisdictions it is considered inadequate. Lobbyists, after all, do not have to pace the halls of legislatures if they want to meet with Parliamentarians. Many lobbyists, in fact, feel that they can easily dispense with meeting with Parliamentarians altogether. As far as they are concerned real power is exercised through the executive and is best approached either at that level or via administrative offices. Conceivably, self-definition could be used to identify lobbyists "creatively loitering" as one lobbyist put it in these offices, but, given the size and extent of most public services, it is much less amenable to control.

German approach

Germany, which is frequently considered the quintessential corporatist state, has, since 1972, required that associations wishing to be heard as the legislature debates changes in policy must **register beforehand, disclosing their specific interests** and the names and addresses of their representatives. Registration is published and secures a pass to the legislature. By 1985, Clarke reported that the register included the names of 1 226 associations and other organisations, but noted that the system had "a far narrower scope than its closest counterparts in Canada and [at that time] Australia and there are no penal sanctions for failing to comply with its provisions" (Clarke, 1991).

This system has been carried over into the reunified Germany, extending to the *Bundestag* and the Federal Government with additional disclosure requirements relating to the number of members and the composition of the board of directors and board of management. According to Malone, the register continues to lack legal force. Its aim:

> ... is to identify clearly lobbyists and interest groups which supply information to the *Bundestag* and its committees. Registration confers no special status or privileges such as an automatic right to be consulted at parliamentary hearings (Clarke, 1991).

The *Bundestag* can refuse to hear registered representatives or can consult with unregistered representatives, so there is **no strong incentive to register**. Furthermore, in an allusion to Germany's corporatist consultation process, Malone notes that "as a substantial number of members of the *Bundestag* are or were members of trade unions or employers' associations, there is inevitably a good deal of political personal contact between such groups and individual members" (Clarke, 1991). In 1996 the annual register contained the names of 1 614 organisations (Crespo Allen, 1996).

According to a 1998 article by Ronit and Schneider, these provisions, and similar arrangements in the German states, have emphasised the representational legitimacy of "peak" associations not only before legislators but at ministry levels where contacts are "most intensive". They maintain that as a result lobbying firms have been discouraged, and that "there is no strong political demand for regulation amongst the political and administrative elites" (Ronit and Schneider, 1998).

Danish experience

A somewhat different impression emerges from a discussion of lobbying in Denmark, which also has a corporatist tradition. Rene Rechtman and Larsen-Ledet report that the corporatist system that prevailed there between the 1940s and 1980s was "sufficiently inclusive and widely understood" that lobby regulation was unnecessary, but that in recent years the intrusion of new players with pluralistic assumptions and the increased use of lobbyists – which had previously not been effective – has suggested the need for oversight and regulation (Larsen-Ledet and Rechtman 1998).

Box 2.4. **Legislating lobbying in North America**

If oversight and regulation is needed, then it may be desirable to meld some of the provisions of North American regulation with those that prevail in corporatist countries. In particular, this would involve a broad definition of who is required to register as a lobbyist. A registry that simply records the names of individuals or organisations who wish to communicate with Parliamentary and Ministry committees does not adequately inform anyone of who is working elsewhere in the government to influence government decisions on behalf of third parties. A registry that includes those lobbyists would not undermine corporatist practices, but could supplement the present system of registering and authorising organisations to participate in formal policy discussions.

These considerations draw attention to the fact that, where the inclusiveness of the registry is concerned, much depends on the legislature's understanding of where lobbying takes place and what activities constitute lobbying. In the United States, for example, federal and state legislation often assumes that lobbying begins and ends at the legislative branch, or, if it takes place elsewhere, with members of the executive who are "covered" in the legislation. Canadian legislation, on the other hand, takes a broader view of how lobbyists target government, extending to nearly all public officials, though contacts with cabinet ministers and senior officials are the subject of more extensive reporting. In today's world, where much government policy is at least shaped, if not resolved upon, at administrative levels, it seems to be essential to employ a broad definition of where lobbying is carried out.

Similarly, it is important to specify what activities constitute lobbying. The popular image of the lobbyist bearding a government official is only partially accurate. When the first Lobbyists Registration Act was debated in Canada, lobbyists argued strenuously that it should cover actual representation, and not the setting up of meetings between clients and officials, or the development for clients of "maps" which traced the development of policy decisions and provided strategies to assist clients to achieve their objectives. At first blush, these appeared to be reasonable limitations on the registration scheme, but experience soon demonstrated that such activities do in fact provide lobbyists with important opportunities to interact with officials and to present arguments that forward their clients' interests. Similarly, it has been necessary to define very narrowly the nature of exchanges between officials and lobbyists over requests for information and apparent administrative issues.

Legal precision

Legal precision is also essential for successful enforcement of regulations. For example, legislation commonly describes lobbyists as communicating with public office holders "in an attempt to influence" (Sections 5.6 and 7 of the Act) decisions. Canadian officials were disappointed to discover that proposed prosecutions had to be abandoned because the Crown Prosecutor concluded that:

> ... in light of the insufficiency of evidence establishing that an attempt to influence had taken place and given there was no probability of obtaining a condemnation, no criminal accusation would be filed...

The focus on the expression "attempt to influence" entails that in order to successfully obtain a prosecution under Sections 5, 6 and 7 one must demonstrate beyond a reasonable doubt that an individual has attempted to influence a public office holder. The criminal nature of the offence requires a very high standard of proof, which is analogous to the standard required to prove the more serious offence of influence peddling under the Criminal Code thereby making it very difficult to secure a conviction under the LRA.[15]

As a consequence of this determination, the references to **attempts to influence were later deleted** from the Canadian Act and lobbying was described in terms of communications "in respect of" legislation, policies and so on.

Local government level

At the local government level, different problems arise. Neighbourhood organisations, comprised almost always of volunteers, are significant actors. Local officials have sought to have the leaders and official representatives of these groups register, but have encountered powerful objections on the grounds that as private citizens acting voluntarily these individuals are exercising constitutional rights that should be not limited by registration. In many cases local activists can point to provisions in the lobby regulations of senior governments that specifically exclude voluntary lobbyists from registration. Quebec addresses this issue through regulation, requiring registration by individuals who perform executive functions for certain interest groups, whether or not they receive compensation.[16]

Exclusions

This brings us to the matter of exclusions. Regardless of how specific laws define lobbyists or the act of lobbying, lawmakers have attempted to achieve greater certainty by setting out exclusions. The most common exclusions refer to the **representatives of other governments** – local, regional and international – who are acting in their official capacities. In addition, it is common to find exclusions that reflect the social and political experience of the jurisdiction. For example, in North America the representatives of formally recognised aboriginal councils are often excluded from the obligation to register [Lobbyists Registration Act Chapter 27, Ontario Statutes, 1998, Section 3 (1)].[17] Certain activities are also excluded, particularly activities of a public nature, such as **appearing before legislative committees** or other inquiries. The principle in both instances has to do with the public role of the official or nature of the activity involved. If either is transparently a performance of a public function, then further publicity, or exposure, is considered to be unnecessary. At the same time, care has to be taken that exclusions are not so broadly stated as to encourage non-compliance. For example, in 1996 the Canadian Lobbyists Registration Act was amended to exclude communications made by lobbyists "in direct response to a written request from a public office holder, for advice or comment" relating to matters before the government (Canadian Government, 1995). It soon became clear that lobbyists could use – or even solicit – requests for comment in such a way that special pleading for their clients could go unreported. Following the next quinquennial review of the Act, the clause was amended so that only communications "restricted to a request for information" could be excluded.[18] Finally, it has to be remembered that the scope of lobbying legislation may create exclusions. That is, what is not specifically covered may be excluded. The US Lobbying Disclosure Act (LDA) of 1995, for example, focuses on contacts between lobbyists and officials and on the expenditures incurred in order to support those contacts. Section 3(7) defines "lobbying activities" as:

> ... lobbying contacts and efforts in support of such contacts, including preparation and planning activities, research and other background work that is intended, at the time it is performed, for use in contacts and co-ordination with the lobbying activities of others.

"Lobbying contacts" are defined in terms of "oral or written communications" to executive or legislative branch officials (Lobbying Disclosure Act of 1995, Public Law 104-65, Section 8). No mention is made of grassroots activities in support of communication with officials, yet this aspect of lobbying is highly developed in the United States and has been recognised in Canada as so much a part of lobbying activity that it must be included in lobbyists' registration filings.[19]

The challenge of definitions

Wording, as always in legislation, determines its effectiveness. Experience has shown that vague or partial definitions of who is to be covered by legislation, or what activities are encompassed, **leads to non-compliance** or inadequate compliance. Therefore:

- The descriptions of lobbyists and of lobbying activity must be clear and unambiguous.
- Equally, exclusions must be precise.

- Definitions must be clearly understood by lobbyists, office holders and members of the public and robust enough to support legal challenges.

For some European countries where globalisation has brought North American lobbying practices into uneasy tension with corporatist processes, it might be advisable to establish **parallel systems of registration**: one dedicated to supporting existing corporatist practices, the other meeting new needs for transparency. Whatever decisions individual legislatures arrive at, it is important to remember that:

- Definitions reflect the broad constitutional and political realities of the country for which they are devised. Therefore, they cannot be transferred from one political system to another without careful consideration and modification.

Where a decision is made to build a registry and regulations around the goal of transparency, effectiveness is most likely to be achieved if there is broad and inclusive definition of:

- Lobbyists and lobbying activities.
- The theatre of lobby activity.

In conclusion, targets for registration are commonly defined in legislation by the fact that they receive compensation for carrying out lobbying activities. Where a definition has eluded lawmakers, lobbyists may be invited to identify themselves by virtue of carrying out specified lobbying activities, though such a procedure can encourage non-compliance. Generally, definitions are refined by specifying that certain classes of actors are excluded from the obligation to register. **These exclusions may reflect constitutional conventions, the political history of the jurisdiction and the practical realities of conducting business between governments.**

Disclosure: How much is enough?

Introduction

A central challenge for this chapter is to identify and articulate those aspects of lobbying activity whose disclosure will, in general, provide officials and the public with sufficient information to satisfy them that lobbyists' activity is compatible with the public interest, and allows parliamentarians to weigh the appeals of lobbyists against advocacy on behalf of ordinary members of the public (Sub-Committee on Bill C-43, p. 20:18).

The challenge in disclosure has to do with the quantity and detail of the information submitted. To achieve transparency there must be **meaningful disclosure**. Both compliance and timely and effective analysis are enhanced if disclosures are pertinent, but parsimonious. Members of the first Canadian parliamentary committee to investigate a proposal to regulate lobbyists confessed that "we have come to realise how difficult it is to achieve transparency while at the same time ensuring that the information desired to accomplish this goal is relevant and produced in a manner which makes it easily understood by the general public, the media and members of Parliament" (Parliament of Canada, 1987). Howard Wilson, speaking from experience, **described the challenge** this way:

> This is the heart of a lobbyist registration system and where the widest range of alternatives is found among different jurisdictions. Where to draw the line can be a matter of considerable difficulty and controversy. Some of the debates in Canada and elsewhere have been driven by the notion that if some disclosed information is good, then more is better. It can, at times, be difficult to keep the debate focused on why lobbyist registration is being considered in the first place, *i.e.* what is the "evil" that is being addressed (OECD, 2006).

Disclosure is the aspect of lobby regulation most susceptible to elaboration, wise and unwise. Initially, Canada's Lobbyists Registration Act, reflecting the Committee concerns previously quoted, made modest demands of registrants. So much so, in fact, that the first version of the Act was derisively called "the business card bill". Subsequent revisions threaten to encumber the registration process, with the most recent requiring lobbyists to make monthly reports of contacts with senior public office holders. Elaboration may flow from experience with lobbying processes and be designed to elicit information that best exposes how governments are influenced, identification of grass-roots and coalition campaigns, for example. However, goaded by evidence of corruption and scandal, **lawmakers sometimes impose ever more exhaustive requirements for disclosure**. Forgetting that the ingenuity of the unscrupulous is inexhaustible, they create thickets of regulation that intimidate all but those they are meant to discourage (OECD, 2006). For example, financial information is a popular target, yet the true costs of a lobbying campaign are extremely difficult to assess. The data demanded is difficult to obtain and what is provided is often incomplete and therefore virtually meaningless.

Core disclosure requirements ask lobbyists to identify:

- the interest being represented;
- the object of lobbying; and
- the government institutions being lobbied.

Each of these categories is susceptible to expansion. Where regulation has been in place for some years, additional disclosure requirements have included spending details, lobbying techniques, organisational membership and, where they are permitted, arrangements for contingency funding. Their usefulness often depends on how legislators intend to apply the information that is collected. If the purpose is primarily to obtain, and to give the public, a broad understanding of what interests will be affected by changes in policy, then general statements may suffice. If, on the other hand, legislators expect that the information might be used in criminal prosecutions, detailed knowledge of lobbyists' activities could be valuable. In the aftermath of the Abramoff scandal, for example, Senator John McCain advocated extending disclosure requirements, arguing that the Federal Bureau of Investigation (FBI) could have identified Abramoff's activities earlier if more information had been available (Continetti, 2006).

The elaboration of core requirements

The following paragraphs will examine the principal disclosure requirements in current legislation. Experience has led to the addition of further categories, these experiences will be considered to draw some general conclusions about their utility and applicability. This section will also look at the disclosure requirements for "dual mandate" lobbyists and at the issues surrounding the timing of reports and the form in which reports are made.

The interest being represented: Cui bono?

While registration identifies lobbyists themselves, it does not **shed much light on those who benefit**. As this became apparent, regulations were introduced that compelled consultant lobbyists to identify the names of their clients, and "any person or organisation that controls or directs the activities of the client or has a direct interest in the outcome of the lobbyist's undertaking" (Government of British Columbia, 2003). In the case of corporations, this would include the names of holding companies or subsidiaries, particularly subsidiaries that, in the language of the US regulations, will benefit from the lobbyists' work. Similar disclosure was required of corporate lobbyists. Some American states go further. New York, for example, demands a copy of the retainer or employment agreement and the names of affiliates. Texas requires associations to describe their methods of decision making, to estimate the number of their members and to name those members who are influential in decision making. Texas also requires lobbyists representing private companies to report the number of shareholders, the officers and/or members of the board of directors and the names of any individuals holding more than 10% of the shares (OECD, 2006).

Lobbying by interest groups has posed more of a challenge. It is not always clear **whether interest group members are the direct beneficiaries of group representations**. The benefits to members may be clear when businesses participate in a trade organisation that lobbies for tariff protection or subsidies, but when organisations representing health professionals lobby for improvements in health care systems the connections are by no means as obvious. They are even more difficult to discern in the lobbying of such public interest groups as Amnesty International. Nevertheless, there is broad support for the contention that however altruistic the origins of lobbying activity, the public interest demands that it should be transparent. In line with this view, the *Green Paper on the European Transparency Initiative* prepared for the European Commission has suggested that groups be asked to explain who they represent, what their mission is and how they are funded.[20]

Legislators have adopted several disclosure mechanisms designed to determine **who is behind lobbying activity**. The United States' federal legislation requires registrants to identify organisations that, in a six month period, contributed more than USD 10 000 to the lobbying activity, or "in whole or in major part plans, supervises or controls" the undertaking [US Public Law 104-65, 109 Stat. 691, ss. 4(b)(3) and (4)]. The Ontario Lobbyists Registration Act, 1998 has a similar requirement for disclosure of the names of those persons or organisations that have contributed more than USD 750 to a lobbying undertaking [Integrity Commissioner and Lobbyists Statute Law Amendment Act, 1998, Ontario Statutes 1998 Chapter 27, ss. 4(7), 5(8) and 6(6)]. While not all Canadian jurisdictions establish a financial threshold for reporting participation in a lobbying undertaking, it is usual to require lobbyists to identify coalition partners and/or to identify entities that have a direct interest in the outcome of the lobby undertaking.

How meaningful is this information? There is no doubt that identification of corporations expecting to benefit from the outcome of lobby undertakings is helpful to officials as they assess the pressures for specific outcomes, and it also **alerts other interests**, including the public, to efforts to obtain public benefits. Similarly, since it is by no means difficult to hide a specific interest behind a real or dummy interest group, it is helpful to require registrants to identify beneficiaries or those who are directing activity. Whether detailed information about private companies or about the decision-making structures of interest groups is truly helpful to policy makers and the public is another matter, and the need for it may in part depend on the availability of such information elsewhere. For example, in many jurisdictions associations are required to file information about their constitutional bylaws, financial structure and leadership in separate registries. It seems counterproductive to burden lobbying databases with information that is available through such sources.

Financial information

Hardened observers of lobbying claim that to **discover who benefits from lobby campaigns, one has to "follow the money"**. It is understandable, therefore, that reporters, politicians and members of the public should attach importance to obtaining information about the costs of lobbying. Intuitively, most observers correlate the level of expenditure on lobbying with the prize to be won, and while this may not be an infallible guide, it is a reasonable assumption. It is also reasonable for the public to question politicians when they appear to be selling public goods too cheaply; industries that are prepared to spend very large sums of money in order to secure favourable public policies may well be expecting to recoup their expenditures at the expense of the taxpayer and consumer. Knowing something of the cost of those campaigns not only alerts the public to the stakes involved [Chenier (ed.), 2003],[21] but also suggests that policy makers should make efforts to discover and consider the preferences of the public at large and of less well-endowed interests.[22] The Alliance for Lobbying Regulation and Ethics Rules in the European Union puts the case for financial closure in the following terms:

- **Financial disclosure greatly enhances the overall transparency on lobbying.** Citizens, as well as journalists and decision-makers, should be able to see how much money is spent overall on lobbying, with the option of breakdowns, *e.g.* per policy area, industry sector or type of lobbying agent.
- **Financial disclosure is needed to fully identify the clients of lobbyists.** If lobbyists only need to list clients but no financial data on them, a disclosure system cannot identify the main actors in strategic alliances or behind front groups. For example: if a company or an association starts a lobbying campaign and enlists a number of other companies or associations who symbolically support that campaign, a system without financial disclosure would fail to capture the key interests behind that campaign. Thus the register would not provide transparency.
- **Financial disclosure helps to identify misleading and unethical lobbying.** Aside from helping to expose misleading lobby campaigns, financial disclosure can also help identify unethical lobbying practices. For example, data from the US lobby disclosure system helped to trigger the investigations into the scandal around lobbyist Jack Abramoff.

Advocates for financial disclosure look to American experience both to support their case and as a source of regulatory models. There, federal regulators began addressing the challenge of disentangling lobby expenditure in 1946 when the Federal Regulation of Lobbying Act was passed, requiring detailed financial information, including:

- The lobbyist's salary and duration of employment.
- How much the lobbyist was paid for expenses and the nature of those expenses.
- Quarterly updating reports were required, specifying: *i)* a "detailed report under oath" of funds received or spent during the preceding quarter; and *ii)* to whom and for what purpose these funds were paid (Congressional Research Service, 1986).
- More detailed reports had to be filed, identifying: *i)* each person making a contribution to the lobbyist or his organisation of USD 500 or more; *ii)* the total sum of all contributions made for the year to date; *iii)* each person who

had been the subject of expenditure USD 10 or more, and the amount, date and purpose of the expenditure; and *iv)* the total sum of expenditure made by or on behalf of any person during the calendar year.

Failure to report this information could bring a fine of up to USD 5 000 or imprisonment for up to a year; conviction of violating the Act might incur larger fines, longer imprisonment and prohibition from lobbying for up to three years.

Box 2.5. **Compliance in reporting on lobbying: Findings of the Socolar report**

Despite the available penalties, Milton J. Socolar, Special Assistant to the Comptroller General, summed up the view of many when he reported to the Senate Subcommittee on Oversight of Government Management in 1991 that the Act "has been largely ineffective". Its failure was largely attributable to the Supreme Court's narrow interpretation of its application; in United States *versus* Harriss (347 US 612) the Court determined that only lobbyists seeking to communicate directly with members of Congress regarding pending or proposed Federal legislation were required to register under the Act. Even so, given the active role members of Congress play in the development of legislation, a considerable number of lobbyists did register and did file reports. The adequacy of the reports, however, left much to be desired. The Socolar group examined the 1989 registrations and found that:

> Information required of registered lobbyists was often submitted late and incomplete. The 6 000 lobbyists reported total receipts of USD 234 million and expenses of USD 76 million for 1989. Some 62% of required reports were filed late in varying degrees and over 90% were incomplete. We could not determine the extent to which required filings were not made, but interviews conducted suggest that there may be a significant number of non-filers.

The enquiry examined 1 107 reports. Of these, 375 (34.9%) disclosed no income nor any disbursements. Nine hundred and five (90.5%) reported neither wages paid nor any fees, salaries or commissions received. Apparently a similar number of the lobbyists filing these reports managed without offices or utilities. Slightly fewer (84.6%) did without telephones, and, 75.1% lobbied without travel, fine dining or entertainment.

The Socolar report did not attribute inadequate reporting exclusively to problems with the financial disclosure requirements. More significant impediments were created by imprecise definitions, inadequate guidance, forms that were "models of confusion" and the lack of effective monitoring; but requirements that left much to the discretion of lobbyists themselves, including those affecting financial disclosure, clearly played their part. In the early years of this era, too, when copying devices were primitive and electronic communication non-existent, the physical impediments to reporting, accessing and storing lobby information would have discouraged lobbyists from registering and members of the media from investigating lobby activity. The General Accounting Office recommended that lobbyists be required to file their contracts and that random audits should be routine.

New Acts

The recommendations of the General Accounting Office were not implemented. Instead after many years of debate and, of course, lobbying, **the 1946 Act was replaced** by the LDA of 1995 (US Public Law 104-65, 109 Stat. 691). The new Act extended coverage so that it clearly included the lobbying of Congressional support staff and executive branch officials "serving in the position of a confidential, policy-determining, policy-making or policy-advocating character" (US House of Representatives, 1995). The Act also attempted to secure meaningful financial information by establishing earnings thresholds to trigger registration and requiring "good faith" estimates of income and expenditures. Lobbying firms were required to register if an undertaking would realise an income, adjusted for inflation, of USD 5 000 or more in a six-month period. Organisations were subject to an expenditure threshold of USD 20 000 for the same period. All registrants had to file semi-annual reports which would include either "good faith" estimates of income and expenditure or a copy of the firm or organisation's filing under the Internal Revenue Code [US Public Law 104-65, 109 Stat. 691, ss. 3 (a), 3 (b)(3) and (4); 5 (3) and (4)].

This attempt to come to grips with the financial aspects of lobbying also encountered difficulties, leading Loree G. Bykerk (2004) to conclude that "many who lobby for organised interests, foreign governments, and corporations do not register even their identity let alone their specific interest or their lobbying expenditures as required by law". Her assessment appeared to be confirmed by a General Accounting Office comparison of LDA "good faith" and Internal Revenue Code filings. It found that the two definitions, having different purposes and therefore different coverage, elicited quite different information, and that lobbyists were able to "switch between ... definition(s) from one year to another, and ... choose the definition that enables (them) to disclose the least information".[23] An amending act later defined more precisely how the definitions were to be used [The Lobbying Disclosure Technical Amendments Act of 1998 (Public Law 105-166)].

Over the last two years, in the wake of a spate of scandals, Congress revisited various lobbying issues, including the problems surrounding financial disclosure. This **re-examination** led in September 2007 to the passage of the Honest Leadership and Open Government Act of 2007 which extensively amended the 1995 act. Two principal changes were made relating to the reporting of income and expenses. The first related to the **timing of reports**. They are to be made quarterly, instead of semi-annually, and 20 days, rather than 45 days, after the beginning of each quarter [Sections 5 (b) 3 and 4]. The second change addresses the **relationship between lobbying and campaign financing**. On a semi-annual basis reports must be filed of contributions made by registered lobbyists to political candidates and organisations (including organisations controlled by the lobbyists, Political Action Committees and party committees). Unlike the reports that are required quarterly, these must specify the date, recipient and amount of the funds involved. Similar records must be filed of expenditures supporting fund-raising events, meetings, retreats and comparable events [Section 5 (d)]. After taking up his office, President Obama immediately issued the Executive Order on Ethics Commitments by Executive Branch Personnel that, for example, includes a ban on "revolving door" practices and lobbyist gifts in the administration.[24]

Usefulness of disclosed information

The **utility of this information can be assessed** by an examination of the websites of the numerous American public interest groups devoted to lobby and election reform. Common Cause, MoveOn, Public Citizen, and the Center for Public Integrity are only a few of the organisations that troll the data available through the Senate Public Records Office and the Federal Election Commission in search of information concerning the pressures exerted on public officials. The database is most effective in identifying the expenditures major interest groups make for advertising, in securing lobby representation, and in supporting friendly politicians. Advocacy groups use it to draw attention to the scale of expenditure by major interests and to their impact on some specific decisions. A typical example of the latter is a study prepared by Public Citizen of a campaign by oil interests to secure nearly a billion dollars in public funding for research into oil extraction from depleted wells; money that Public Citizen argued the oil companies could easily afford from their own coffers. The study traced the role of a Clinton-era official in spearheading the lobby campaign and the flow of money to a campaign fund supporting Representative Tom DeLay. The oil consortium achieved its objectives when a late-night amendment was added to an energy bill (O'Donnell, 2007).

Clearly the LDA contributes to transparency at the federal level in the American policy process. The recent revisions should enhance efforts to track lobbying activity in a timely fashion and shed new light on the relations between lobbyists and lawmakers. However, there are good reasons for asking whether the American approach is applicable elsewhere.

US particularities

Because the American legislative system invests individual lawmakers with an unusual degree of influence over legislation, an environment is created in which lobbying of senior executive branch officials and members of Congress is not only much more extensive but also more open than is the case in many other countries, where the executive is usually the principal and often the exclusive source of legislative and policy change. Lobbying legislators in those systems is far less effective than lobbying the cabinet and the public service.

The **American electoral system is also quite different** from the systems that prevail in many other jurisdictions. It places a premium on securing financial support from the public, whereas in many other systems strict limits are placed on financial contributions made by voters or organisations and on campaign spending. Frequently, too, public financing of elections is the norm. Elsewhere, then, depending on the structure of the electoral system involved, the close connection between lobbying and campaign financing may be regulated most effectively through elections acts.

Finally, the **American emphasis on pluralism** produces an array of watch-dog groups strongly supported by foundations and donations from citizens. These groups are extremely active in monitoring lobby activity in general and in specific policy fields. Their vigilance compensates for the fact that the government's own administrative support for lobby regulation is extremely modest. In 1995, for example, the House Judiciary Committee in recommending adoption of the LDA estimated that it would cost only USD 500 000 a year, a minuscule amount in comparison to the scale of the lobbying industry itself; in 1975 Washington lobbyists were reported to be earning USD 100 million a year, a figure that had risen to USD 2.5 billion by 2006.[25] A record USD 3.28 billion was spent on lobbying at the federal level in the United States in 2008, employing almost 15 000 registered lobbyists.[26] Lobbying expenditure also showed significant increase at the state level, for example it exceeded USD 270 million in California and USD 150 million in New York, with over 3 000 registered lobbyists for each state in 2006.[27] Civil society in most countries does not yield an array of watch-dog groups that can match America's. Elsewhere, then, the task of monitoring, analysing and publicising data generated through financial disclosure must fall to governmental regulatory bodies which are seldom accorded the resources needed to analyse and investigate complex financial data.

Canadian case

The Canadian case illustrates this point. When the Federal Parliament first considered lobby regulation these **significant differences** led a bi-partisan group of Canadian MPs to recommend against requiring financial disclosure. They met with registry officials in Washington DC, and Sacremento, California, and heard testimony from various groups on the issue. Even the Coalition on Acid Rain, a Canadian-based environmental group active in the United States, which was sympathetic to requiring financial disclosure, warned against creating a burdensome reporting process. The Coalition reviewed for the Committee, the various forms required by the US registration process and demonstrated the financial and other burdens imposed by that system.[28] Other groups also dwelt on these difficulties. The Canadian Medical Association (CMA) reported, typically:

> The CMA would find it very difficult to accurately report on the amount spent on lobbying unless the term was more specifically defined. We could report on the costs of CMA only activities where they have a direct, vested interest for the Association or its members – for example, the Association's lobby activities for increased tax deductible registered retirement saving plan contributions. But, it was not possible to accurately report on the cost of activities of local branches of the Associations, provincial divisions, specialty bodies, CMA Councils and Committees, staff, etc., that have bearing on CMA advice and input to government on a myriad of activities such as the control of the medical manpower supply or the Medical and Health Advisory Committee of the Correctional Service of Canada.[29]

For regulators, these difficulties pale in comparison to the issues that emerge when a broad-based, long-term lobbying campaign is examined. A good example is the battle over tobacco regulation which has been waged in many countries since the 1960s. Both industry and health lobbies have formed coalitions – some of them extensive – whose members engage in a variety of activities ranging from sponsoring and collating scientific research through to organizing grass-roots campaigns aimed at influencing various levels of government, engaging in direct lobbying, advertising widely, sponsoring sympathetic groups, organising conferences, mass protests and petitions, mounting press campaigns, engaging in litigation and in recent years utilising the Internet.[30] Tracking the expenditures involved in these lobbying exercises is a forensic, as well as a regulatory, challenge.

Such considerations, together with the fact that the government of the day was known to favour only a limited budget for the Lobbyists Registration Branch, convinced the Canadian Parliamentary Committee that **meaningful financial disclosure was out of the question**; and that the complexities of analysing and monitoring financial disclosure were such that the cost of the effort involved far outweighed the benefits. That view still prevails at the federal level in Canada and in all the provinces that regulate lobbying, except Quebec where the Lobbying Transparency and Ethics Act requires that consultant lobbyists identify which of four compensation zones each specific undertaking will realise.[31] According to the Commissioner of Lobbyists, André Côté, this information is used as an indication of the significance that a client attaches to a specific lobbying campaign.[32]

This implies that **other** disclosure requirements and other forms of lobby regulation may be just as useful as financial disclosure. In this context it is interesting to note that the recent American reforms paid more attention to prohibiting specific lobbying activities than they did to financial disclosure.

Box 2.6. **Enhancing transparency: Role of financial disclosure**

Nevertheless, a case can still be made for requiring financial disclosure. Regulation of election spending, for example, may not entirely preclude the disclosure of lobbyists' involvement in campaigns, some aspects of which may have financial implications. The fact that much public policy is derived from advice provided by the administrative branch does not ensure that interests will not invest in **expensive lobbying campaigns**. On the contrary, indirect lobbying that mobilises public opinion to sway ministerial decisions is often employed to offset the advice of officials and is seldom cheap. The organisation and nature of campaigns may change, but they can still be very expensive, as is illustrated by our earlier reference to the struggles over tobacco regulation. It is important to know, then, what moneys are expended to influence the public. Finally, power, whether it is exercised by legislators or by cabinet ministers or officials, is always susceptible to corruption, and therefore not only warrants vigilant enforcement of anti-bribery laws but also the application of regulations, such as financial disclosure, that help to expose corruption.

These and other considerations indicate that **some financial disclosure is desirable**. What is being suggested here, though, is that its value should not be exaggerated and that the American approach, while suited to political processes in the United States, may have to be greatly modified if it is applied elsewhere. Regulation is most effective when it is fashioned to reflect how policy is made and where pressure is most likely to be applied. For example, whether the Quebec approach provides adequate information is a good point, but it does recognise that because policy making in that jurisdiction has characteristics that are different from those in the United States, attempts to determine how money influences public policy should also have a different character. The same is true of lobby regulation at the federal level in Canada. There the executive dominates policy formation and disclosure has to focus not on attempts to influence individual legislators, as it does in the United States, but on the relationships between lobbyists and influential officials on the one hand, and on the myriad ways in which public opinion is moulded on the other.

Gift-giving, travel supported by lobbyists, social events and spousal lobbying have been increasingly limited. Effective **revolving door regulations, election act prohibitions**, disclosure of all communications with senior officials, disclosure of previous government employment and political party positions, the banning of contingency fees, the use of codes embedded in legislation and stern sanctions against bribery may be sufficient to illuminate the intense lobbying of the relatively small pool of politicians and officials at the centre, and to discourage corruption. Critics might suggest that not all of these measures enhance transparency. Many of them do, however, and others address equally important goals of eliminating corruption and fostering openness in government. On the other hand, transparency could be more effectively enhanced in many jurisdictions if more attention were to be paid to the financial outlays involved in influencing public opinion.

To sum up: one can say that in most jurisdictions the effectiveness of financial disclosure should not be exaggerated, and though it is a useful part of lobby regulation it is most useful when its design and implementation reflect the policy-making system that it is meant to monitor and serve.

Objects of lobbying

Unquestionably, the public and officials need to know what it is that lobbying campaigns are intended to achieve. In many instances, protagonists are only too eager to **identify their causes**, but in others they have strong reasons for obscuring their objectives. Their motives are not necessarily illicit; probably most reflect competitive pressures in business. It is said that the Canadian data on lobby registration is followed most avidly not by politicians, officials or journalists, but by lobbyists themselves, because they find in it useful indications of the work that their competitors are doing and the opportunities that businesses are pursuing.[33]

This poses a dilemma for registry officials: how precise should the demand be for information concerning the objects of lobbying? Too precise, and the unintended effect is to damage enterprise. Too vague, and the public interest is violated. The LDA of 1995 captures the sense of this dilemma when it prescribes that the registrant must provide a statement of "the general issue areas in which the registrant expects to engage" and:

> … to the extent practicable, specific issues that have (as of the date of the registration) already been addressed or are likely to be addressed in lobbying activities [Sections 4 (b) (5) (a) and (b)].

The Canadian legislation is less sympathetic. It requires "particulars to identify the subject matter in respect of which the individual undertakes to communicate with a public office holder or to arrange a meeting, and any other information respecting the subject-matter that is prescribed", and goes on to demand "particulars to identify any relevant legislative proposal, Bill, resolution, regulation, policy or programme, grant, contribution, financial benefit or contract" [Lobbyists Registration Act (Consolidation of March 2005), Sections 5 (2) (g) and (h)]. In its advice to lobbyists the Registration Branch indicates that in addition to **specifying the object of lobbying** by precise name and number, registrants should also give "a brief description… as to why you are lobbying with reference to the above-mentioned Act, Legislation, Bills, etc. (*e.g.* with respect to its implementation and/or review of…)".[34]

The information thus elicited varies widely. Consider, for example, recent registrations by Queen's University and the University of Calgary, two academic institutions with comparable interests. The President of Queen's University, the signing officer for the registration, reported that the University expected to lobby in relation to "public policy, Canada research chairs, student assistance and financial support for higher education, immigration policy, commercialisation, indirect funds for research, copyright reform, intellectual property, tax reform, charitable donations, land acquisition, health sciences initiatives". One can imagine senior members of the university administration brain-storming to come up with this list, which by no means covers the full gamut of policies that Canadian universities are concerned with. The University of Calgary opted for a more succinct statement, proposing to lobby in relation to "post-secondary education, funding, research and development, climate change technology, sustainable development and innovation". It is unlikely that the University of Calgary is any less interested than Queen's University in immigration policy (as it relates to students and the hiring of staff) or that Queen's, which for a number of years has been working to develop a solar-powered automobile, would neglect policy issues related to "climate change technology and sustainable development and innovation".

All of which illustrates the **difficulty of providing meaningful responses to disclosure requirements**, and suggests that it would be more sensible to assume as some European practices appear to do, that simply stating the lobbyist's sphere of interests is sufficient to alert observers to the ramifications of a lobby undertaking.[35] That is, until one begins to analyse some of the responses provided by lobbyists acting for more specialised organisations. Here two strategies may be adopted. On the hand, the registrant may present a long list of legislation, or programmes, that are the object of lobbying activity, hoping thereby to hide the central purpose of the campaign in a mass of detail. On the other, a terse description – such as the recent filing on behalf of a technology group, which stated only that the group would be lobbying on "Canada's innovation strategy" and "meetings" – is no more revealing.[36] It may be that the difficulty of communicating a complex assignment on a short electronic form, rather than obfuscation, explains why these entries are vague and meaningless. At any rate, it justifies the authority given to officials to require registrants to provide more complete information.

As a general conclusion, lawmakers have a **choice between accepting broad descriptions of lobbyists' objectives or requiring them to provide more precise details** about the specific legislation, programme, policy or other government activity that they are concerned with. If the former, legislators must expect that interests will state their objectives in very broad terms, often with the result that it is virtually impossible to discern the real purpose of a lobby campaign. American and Canadian law attempts to force more meaningful disclosure by first asking for a general statement on the issue area, and then requiring information about the specific legislation, policy or benefit that the undertaking addresses. The information thus provided may not be illuminating. American laws are more likely to require the filing of contracts and other documents. It may be that truly meaningful disclosure can only be obtained through a combination of these requirements. That is, the current succinct reports that are filed on forms, if coupled with a requirement to file certain documents, and with the authority on the part of registry officials to demand clarification and/or to conduct investigations, may ensure that meaningful information will ultimately be provided.

It must be remembered that disclosure in and of itself cannot fully inform either officials or the general public of the purpose or processes of a lobbying campaign. The key to effective disclosure lies in the **lawmakers' understanding of what information is needed to shed light on the policy ramifications of a lobbying campaign**, and to alert officials to illicit lobbying activities. To secure the latter objective, registry officials must have the authority to demand that registrants clarify their filings and to pursue investigations further, if necessary, to the point of setting in motion full-fledged criminal enquiries. To achieve the former objective two conditions are necessary: registry officials need the authority to demand clarification of filings, and there must be in place both an informed bureaucracy, and a segment of the public – amongst journalists, advocacy groups and rival interests – equipped to understand the implications of the information provided, and to lead a public debate on the issues that it raises.

The targets of lobbying

Lobby registration requirements will seek to **identify the points in decision-making processes where lobbyists have attempted to exert influence**. However, there is a good deal of variation in the amount of information required and in the coverage of governmental institutions. European registries appear to most frequently require lists of interests seeking to appear before specific parliamentary and administrative committees. The United States LDA describes reportable "lobbying contacts" as "any oral or written communication ... to a covered executive branch official or a covered legislative branch official" made on behalf of a client. However, in their semi-annual reports lobbyists must provide lists of the Houses of Congress and the federal agencies contacted on behalf of clients [Sections 3(8) (a) and 5 (b) (2) (B)].[37] Canada's Lobbyists Registration Act treats almost the entire public service as susceptible to lobbying influence [Section 2(1)], and requires lobbyists to identify on first registration "any department or other governmental institution" with which they communicate or intend to communicate [Section 5(2)].

In the past Canada's federal legislation did not require lobbyists to **name the officials** that they contact. Even when lobbyists made contact with officials at social events, they did not have to name the officials, but to report "informal communications" with unnamed officials of specified agencies. However, the new Federal Accountability Act (FAA) now requires lobbyists in Ottawa to identify any senior public office holders (designated public office holders) with whom they communicate. Senior public office holders are ministers of the Crown, deputy ministers, associate and assistant deputy ministers and similar designated officials. This information must be filed monthly and must include the date of communications and "any particulars ... to identify the subject matter of the communication" [The Federal Accountability Act, Statutes of Canada, 55 Eliz. II, 2006, Chapter 9, Sections 67 (2) and 69 (4)]. This is by far the most searching disclosure requirement of any lobby regulation currently in effect, and it will be interesting to see whether it does indeed provide meaningful information to policy makers, the media, and the parliamentary opposition on the one hand or the general public on the other. One can envisage the public obtaining a very clear understanding of the frequency with which lobbyists interact with senior officials and when interaction occurs. Doubtless, too, this information, if properly reported, could assist in prosecutions in lobbying cases. By the same token interactions between officials and lobbyists may become increasingly formal, as both strive to avoid any appearance of undue influence. On the other hand, administration of the reporting process will be onerous. *The Lobby Monitor* predicts that:

> ... if it is like many of the other "sunshine laws", it is quite likely that it will succumb to one of two problems – relevant information (purposefully) buried amidst a sea of useless and irrelevant information, or, information so truncated as to barely meet the letter, but not the spirit, of the law... (*The Lobby Monitor*, 2006).

Other possible outcomes include engaging in "non-reportable contact by pushing the point of contact below the required reporting levels in departmental hierarchies" or to rely on "serendipitous" meetings with targeted officials. Alternatively, the *Monitor* wonders whether senior officials will be inundated with communications from lobbyists whose clients insist that they leave no public office holder in the dark about their needs. In the final analysis, the *Monitor* expects the reporting requirements to be expressed so vaguely that they allow "for as much ambiguity and anonymity as possible", so that "after much money, time and effort, when all is in place, the public is likely to be left slightly poorer but none the wiser". This could well be the case. On the other hand, the FAA also provides that the Commissioner of Lobbyists shall have greater independence than earlier officials were given. Consequently, lobbyists may discover that it is not as easy as it has been to secure loosely-worded regulations.

Before leaving this subject, it should be noted that **lobby regulations generally exempt certain types of communication from reporting**. All the North American legislation examined for this study exempts formal presentations to legislative and other hearings that are on the public record. Communications asking for information or related to specific issues of enforcement or interpretation are also exempt. Lawyers advising their clients "on the construction, meaning, or legislative or administrative action", to quote Hawaii's lobbying manual, are usually exempt, unless the communication is deemed to be an attempt to lobby [*Lobbying Restrictions and Reporting Manual for the Lobbyists Law*, Chapter 97, Hawaii Revised Statutes, Section 3 (5)]. Some jurisdictions exempt communications responding to requests for information from public servants. Draft legislation recently introduced in Alberta does this, but Parliamentarians in Ottawa have concluded that such requests are susceptible to connivance between officials and lobbyists and treat them as lobbying communications [Section 4 (2) (c)].[38] Most of these exemptions are meant to cover communications that are on the public record, relate to the specific application of regulations, emanate from lawyer-client relations or involve requests for information. However, depending on the precision with which the exemption is worded, it is sometimes possible for skilled lobbyists to use these communications to, in effect, lobby. An apparently innocuous request for information, for example, may encourage a public official to purse a course action favoured by the lobbyist.

Other disclosure requirements

Understanding of the policy implications of lobbying undertakings can be significantly enhanced when the names of clients and other potential beneficiaries are known. **Identification of the institutions being lobbied is equally important**, since it allows tracking of decision processes, and alerts officials and others to the need to ensure that all issues and considerations are taken into account. However, other information is sometimes required, the salience of which is not always clear. Although these requirements may have been injected into the regulatory process as a result of particular situations, they can acquire a life of their own, becoming virtually permanent fixtures, regardless of their true utility or the fact that they may unnecessarily encumber both regulation and analysis.

Broadly speaking, these additions have two purposes. First, they are believed to **shed light on the impact lobbying has on decision making**. Second, they may reinforce other regulations. A few serve both purposes.

In the first category one finds, in American legislation, the requirement that **foreign interests** should be identified. This requirement has its origins in the Foreign Agents Registration Act of 1938 which required individuals, other than diplomatic representatives, who were acting for foreign governments, political parties, corporations or other organisations by spreading propaganda or otherwise engaging in political activities. The Act was later amended to shift its focus to the gathering of information on lobbyists representing foreign corporations, and, in 1995, incorporated into the LDA, a step that possibly reflects the declining utility of such information in an age when most domestic economic policy has to take account of global economic conditions (US General Accounting Office, 1990). Canada's Lobbyists Registration Act imposes a very different requirement when it calls for disclosure of:

> ... particulars to identify any communication technique that the individual uses or expects to use in connection with the communication with the public office holder, including any appeals to members of the public through the mass media or by direct communication that seek to persuade those members of the public to communicate directly with a public office holder in an attempt to place pressure on the public office holder to endorse a particular opinion [Sections 5 (2) (j) and 7 (3) (k)].

By identifying **grassroots campaigns** that have been fomented by lobbyists, legislators presumably hoped that policy makers would be able to distinguish the "genuine article". Given that the sophistication of modern lobbying makes it unlikely that any significant campaign will lack either professional lobbyists or grassroots campaigning, this hope has probably proven unrealistic, and the information the provision generates may be of greater interest to students of lobbying than to policy makers. Nevertheless, the clause does provide other benefits, notably, the fact that it enables officials to elicit reports of "unofficial" communications at, for example, social occasions, conferences and so on.

Disclosure requirements that reinforce or complement other regulations would include those that call for:

- details of previous government employment and public office holding;
- contingency contracts; and
- government funding.

The first reinforces moratoria on lobbying by former office holders. The second may alert finance officials to infringements of regulations governing the awarding of contracts when contingency fees are involved, and the last reflects regulations that prohibit government agencies from attempting to lobby for preferred policies.

Disclosure of lobbying from within

Lobbying by legislators

The term "**dual-mandate lobbying**" may have originated in Sweden where, according to the European Parliament's report on rules on lobbying and inter-groups in the national parliaments of the member states, there is some discussion about the dangers of a "dual mandate" for MPs involved in interest groups or state authorities. This is an issue that has been touched on earlier, in comparing the status of interest groups in corporatist countries with their counterparts in pluralist states. Although in Sweden this debate appears not to have altered the status quo, in some other countries it has brought about changes in the way legislators disclose their relations with groups.

The central issue is whether a legislator who represents a constituency is subject to a **conflict of interest** when he or she also acts as a representative of a collective body, such as a union or an employers association. In France, deputies in the National Assembly are expressly required to use their positions exclusively to carry out their public duties, and are forbidden to belong to "any association or group which defends private, local or professional interests" or to make "any commitments to such groups regarding their parliamentary activities, if such membership or commitments involve accepting mandatory instructions" (Malone, 2004). As already pointed out, other European countries have taken an entirely different approach. Germany, Sweden and Denmark have not only considered the representation of collective bodies to be compatible with election to the legislature, they treat it as being in the public interest, since it contributes to the development of consensus on major policies. This understanding probably accounts for the fact that there appear to be no rules governing disclosure of member's interests.

The debate on the issue in the United Kingdom illustrates its complexities. It waxed and waned for many years, and, according to Grant Jordan (1998), came close, in the 1990s, to ushering in full-fledged lobbying legislation. Lobbyists themselves were reported to be in favour of such a step, but "unexpectedly" the push for legislation gave way to "regulation of legislators, rather than lobbyists". **Members of Parliament had represented special interests for generations**, and there was resistance to attempts to limit their activities. However, the debate over consultancies was fuelled by a series of scandals involving lobbying, and gradually controls were imposed. These took the form of resolutions on the conduct of members, the setting up of committees on standards, and the establishment of a register of members interests which would record all outside sources of remuneration which involved "the provision of services in their capacity as members of Parliament" (Allen, 1996). On 6 November 1995, the House passed a resolution relating to "conduct of members" and prohibiting paid advocacy relating to certain situations. As with earlier resolutions, the general prohibition it enunciated was tempered by subsequent elaboration:

> ... in particular no members of the House shall, in consideration of any remuneration, fee, payment, or reward or benefit in kind, direct or indirect, which the member or any member of his or her family has received, is receiving or expects to receive: *i)* advocate or initiate any

> cause or matter on behalf of any outside body or individual; or *ii)* urge any other member of either House of Parliament, including ministers, to do so, by means of any speech, question, motion, introduction of a bill or amendment to a motion or a bill (Allen, 1996).

In other words, while the members were **constrained against engaging in debate on behalf of outside interests**, they were not forbidden to lobby informally for those interests. Consequently, the rules on members disclosure continued to be enforced and were strengthened, providing for declaration of interest in respect of matters coming before the House; the deposit with the Commissioner for Standards of agreements involving the provision of services by members in their Parliamentary capacity and prohibiting members from initiating, participating in, or attending delegations to ministers or public officials where issues would be addressed that relate exclusively to the organisation with which the member has a paid interest. They also required members to report directorships and consultancies and other professional undertakings where they might receive remuneration in return for offering guidance concerning the lobbying of members, ministers and officials (Allen, 1996).

According to the Sixth Report of the Committee on Standards in Public Life, these measures have "**dramatically changed the perception of lobbying among MPs**":

> Our witnesses were overwhelmingly of the opinion that the regulation of MPs through the ban on paid advocacy and the new rules on registration of interests had changed the approach in Westminster for the better. The assessment of the former Parliamentary Commissioner for Standards was reassuring:
>
> "To the best of my knowledge the financial links with lobbyists have now been broken. Some non-financial links are proving embarrassing but at least the spectre of cash for influence through this route has fallen away."[39]

To summarise: in addition to prohibiting the direct and formal advocacy by members and their participation in certain types of meetings, the British House of Commons requires members to register and deposit agreements whereby they provide services arising out of their Parliamentary capacity, including advisory undertakings, and to declare their interest in matters coming before the House.

Lobbying by family members, legislative staff and journalists

The United Kingdom has also dealt with the issue of lobbying by members' support staff, who, because they hold full passes to the Palace of Westminster, have relatively **free access to members** and could be in a position to exert influence. Registers were established for staff members and journalists, requiring the latter to report "both the employment for which they received the pass and any other paid occupation or employment where their privileged access to Parliament may be relevant", and staff members to register "any relevant gainful occupation" – that is occupations that "might reasonably be thought to be advantaged in any way by access to the parliamentary buildings and their services and facilities". Staff members must also report the receipt of gifts (Allen, 1996).

In recent years lobbying by family members has become an issue. In Washington DC, where marriages between lawmakers and lobbyists are not uncommon, the Senate recently adopted an ethics package that, *inter alia*, will **prevent spouses from taking advantage of their family status to lobby** members of Congress (Kirkpatrick, 2006; Birnbaum and Weisman, 2007).

Disclosure requirements for "All-Party Groups"

The growth of executive power and the consequent decline of influence on the part of back-bench members of legislatures have led to the evolution of members' groups to informally examine broadly-defined issue areas. The composition and concerns of these groups vary according to the public agenda and that of members. They may be referred to as "All-Party Groups", Parliamentary Groups, Parliamentary Caucus Groups or as Inter-groups, and their organisation and proceedings are not highly institutionalised.

Where these groups are composed entirely of legislators who are independent of any interest, and where they receive staff support from officials of the legislature itself, their presence and activities must be treated as part of the normal functioning of the legislature. However, when these groups admit members who are not legislators or when they receive staff support from outside interests, questions arise about their susceptibility to influence.

Westminster requires groups whose members are drawn from more than one party to register the names of the officers of the group and the source and extent of any benefits that they receive, including "the provision of staff help by outside organisations or individuals" and relevant occupational information relating to outside staff (Allen, 1996). The **groups must also adhere to Parliamentary rules** governing their organisation, membership and influence by outside interests. Although currently the British Parliament appears to be the only legislature that has articulated rules to deal with this issue, the Committee on Constitutional Affairs of the European Parliament has recently proposed a resolution that calls for "clarity" on intergroups in the form of a list of registered and non-registered intergroups on Parliament's website, including declarations of the financial interests of their chairs, (European Parliament, 2007).

Disclosure: Balancing openness and efficacy

In conclusion, disclosure is a key building block to enhance transparency in lobbying. Disclosure is also the soft under-belly of lobby regulation. Effective disclosure requirements elicit that information which most **succinctly and accurately**:

- captures the intent of lobbying activity;
- identifies its beneficiaries; and
- points to those offices and institutions that are its targets.

Even when regulation succeeds in securing this core information, it will by no means ensure that decision processes are transparent or satisfy the legitimate information needs of key players in the legislative process. Depending on those needs, **supplementary disclosure will be required**. Legislators and ministers, for example, will want to know where lobbying pressure is coming from, and whether it reflects broad public opinion. Consequently they have an interest in securing the disclosure of information about coalitions and about techniques of lobbying that generate grassroots support. They also have an interest in ascertaining where information is coming from and whether it is credible, but for policy analysts that information is central to their concerns. Watchdogs for the public – and for other interests – insist on disclosure that reveals where lobbyists have been heard, and the relative attention paid to competing camps. Finally, the official guardians of public integrity will want records that assist them to track illicit lobbying undertakings. Attempts to satisfy even these users of disclosed information – and they are by no means the only ones asking for expanded disclosure – can create a reporting system that collapses under its own weight.

Given this inclination toward the infinite expansion of disclosure requirements, regulators have to remember that while much is feasible, it is important to apply a few **basic rules**, namely:

- Information sought and collected has to be **relevant** to the core goals of ensuring transparency, integrity and efficacy.
- The demand for information is **realistic** in practical and legal terms.
- Information can be **disseminated** efficiently to the public, to legislators and to officials.

Information needs that require a less frugal approach might be served in the following ways. Where transparency is a prime concern, but regulators apprehend that the public, including the media, will be overwhelmed by data, supplementary information could be made available through **hyperlinks**. Where prosecution is contemplated, documentation and extensive records are essential. In these circumstances, regulation may be best served if lobbyists are required to **hold records** for a given period, or file them in a separate process.

To reinforce all disclosure requirements, registry officials must have authority to call for clarification of filings, to carry out further investigations, and to hand off enquiries to the police.

Finally, it should be noted that disclosure on the part of legislators who are permitted to lobby has to observe somewhat different rules than those imposed on others. A member of a legislature has privileges and opportunities denied to others. Therefore, he or she has a **particular obligation** to reveal any undertakings with outside interests that stem specifically from the member's role as a legislator. Similar obligations apply to legislative staff and to parliamentary journalists.

Reporting processes and technologies

Lobby regulation has engaged the interest of legislatures in much of Europe and North America, but, as already mentioned, the adoption of regulatory measures has occurred sporadically. The measures themselves are by no means uniform, and their administration frequently reflects the idiosyncrasies of the adopting legislatures. For example, separate registries may exist for each legislative chamber. Some registries are accessible through the Internet, and filing itself can be conducted electronically. For example, the Australian Government Lobbyists Register[40] is a public document that contains information about lobbyists who make representations to the government on behalf of their clients. Others seem to rely on the provision of documents that are not amenable to website reporting.

Electronic filing and reporting

Nevertheless, the current interest in lobby regulation has been accompanied by a growing appreciation of the utility of electronic filing and reporting. Electronic filing has made possible the collection or dissemination of far more information than the early regulators of lobbying could have imagined. Essentially, **electronic filing has made modern regulation feasible**. Its benefits are numerous:

- Registrants can file efficiently from their offices.[41]
- Forms can elicit quantifiable information, thereby facilitating analysis.
- Information can be easily stored, and archival and documentation storage costs are greatly reduced.
- Internet access to filings and reports eliminates the physical centralisation of information and makes that information readily available to members of the public as well as officials, thereby facilitating transparency.

At the same time, electronic management of lobby records may impede transparency. This is especially true of forms calling for disclosure of information concerning the objects of lobbying undertakings. Clearly, registry officials have had to acquire experience in developing forms that elicit truly informative responses, and where such information is not forthcoming officials need the authority to investigate.

In addition, electronic filing cannot meet all the information needs of lobby regulation. Although it is relatively easy to file contracts, agreements and other business document electronically, legislators have to consider when it is lawful or in the **public interest** to make that information publicly available. It may be more appropriate to hold some information in confidence, or to require registrants and their clients to retain records against the demands of some future inquiry.

Information overload can also be a problem. As some lobbyists have discovered, **providing too much information can obscure lobbying objectives** just as effectively as providing too little. Well-intentioned data collection can be equally unhelpful. Detailed expense accounts, for example, may ultimately tell very little, and the filing of voluminous records of meetings, official and unofficial, between senior office holders and lobbyists may yield little useful information to all but the most persistent and experienced enquirers. Requiring registrants and their clients to deposit or retain this kind of information may facilitate the policing of the lobby activity, and perhaps, therefore, is necessary. However, its inclusion on registry websites may simply inhibit the public from enquiring into lobbying activities that should be transparent. If legislators decide to add appreciably more disclosure requirements to registries, they may find it helpful to establish two-tier sites so that summary information can be supplemented by more extensive reporting accessed through hyperlinks.

In short, electronic filing has greatly facilitated lobby registration and regulation. However, there are limits to its application. Although the technology can handle incredible amounts of data, the human capacity to access it still has limits and the ingenuity of individuals who wish to obscure their undertakings is correspondingly extensive. Hence, administrators of registry processes must be ingenious in developing forms that elicit genuinely useful information and legislators must avoid expanding demands for information to the point where it is difficult for the public to digest. Supplementary methods of holding and accessing information and documentation are essential, as are provisions in the regulations that allow registry officials to require further information and to carry out investigations.

Timeliness

Reporting deadlines are as important as disclosure itself. To serve the public interest, disclosure must be made and updated in a **timely fashion**. Canada's federal law requires initial reporting within ten days of entering into a lobbying undertaking [Lobbyists Registration Act (2004), Section 5 (1.1)], and the American law, 45 days (The Lobbying Disclosure Act of 1995, Section 4 a.1). In Washington DC, registrants must file reports semi-annually updating the information initially provided, but in Ottawa the new FAA requires monthly reporting on certain activities, such as communication with senior public office holders.[42]

Codes of conduct

Codes of conduct have increasingly become a part of modern lobby regulation. Three types of conduct now affect the operations of lobbyists in a number of countries.

The least coercive are the **professional codes** adopted in several jurisdictions by associations that have been organised **by lobbyists** themselves. These associations represent lobbyists to government and to other business sectors. They attempt in various ways to enhance the professional calibre of the lobbying community, conducting training sessions and developing codes of professional conduct which to some extent emulate the codes that govern the traditional professions. These efforts are constrained by the nature of the lobbying business itself. Unlike medicine, law, architecture or engineering, lobbying is a field of endeavour that can be entered relatively easily. It does not require a long period of formal study; there are no vetting bodies to confer credentials on new lobbyists. Furthermore, no legislature has conferred on these embryo professional bodies the same legal disciplinary powers held by the senior professions. There is, in effect, no compulsion to belong to a professional body in order to practice. The fact that many lobbyists belong to the legal profession also hampers efforts to create and impose on practitioners a single professional identity. Consequently, though some associations of lobbyists have attempted to discipline wayward practitioners,[43] the open nature of the business and public ignorance of professional codes has rendered their efforts largely ineffective. The codes, therefore, state important ground rules for lobbyists in their relations with one another, with clients and with government officials, but because enforcement is extremely limited they do little to constrain those lobbyists who wish to break the rules.

Employment and post-employment codes and the rules governing the conduct of members of legislatures are in several ways more significant influences on the behaviour of lobbyists. A condition of obtaining access to the European Parliament, for example, is that lobbyists must "comply strictly" with the rules that require members to report remuneration or other benefits, including staff assistance, provided by third parties, and must satisfy themselves that the appropriate report has been registered.[44] They must also comply with staff regulations governing the employment of former officials and respect rules relating to the conduct of members and of members' assistants. A number of jurisdictions now have rules in place that purport to regulate the conduct of members of the legislature and public servants, and though lobbyists may not be specifically enjoined to respect them, the consequences of ignoring them, as far as public officials are concerned, will act as a constraint on their behaviour and thus on that of lobbyists.

A few jurisdictions **impose codes of conduct on lobbyists**, either as a condition of access to legislatures and government offices, or as in the case of Canada, as part of the legislation regulating lobbying. As already mentioned, the European Parliament, under Rule 9(4), permits lobbyists to hold permanent passes to the legislature on condition that they observe a code of conduct. Some aspects of the code have been noted. Others require lobbyists to disclose to the members and other officials that they deal with the interests that they represent, and to refrain from certain activities.[45] Failure to comply with the code can lead to withdrawal of the lobbyist's pass, and thus to denial of access to Parliament.

Some American states also couple lobbyist registration with formal or *de facto* codes. Iowa, for example, does not have a code, but prohibits lobbyists from intentionally deceiving public officials with regard to facts pertinent to lobbying; sending unauthorised communications to public officials, accepting contingency fees, or acting as a conduit for campaign funds. Wilson notes that in California "every person who registers as a lobbyist... must periodically attend a lobbyist ethics orientation course", which is conducted by the ethics committees of the state legislature. Certification as a lobbyist is contingent on taking the course. Wilson also notes that the state of Texas has adopted a code of conduct for lobbyists, but that it is primarily concerned with the lobbyist's relationship with clients (OECD, 2006).

Legislating code of conduct: Canada

Canadian governments appear to be the only ones who **legislate codes of conduct**. Amendments to the Lobbyists Registration Act which came into effect in 1996 authorised the Ethics Counsellor to develop a code that would apply to all registrants and in-house lobbyists [Section 10 (2) (1)].[46] Quebec and Newfoundland subsequently introduced similar provisions.[47] The Code, which came into effect in 1997, has two elements, a statement of principles and a set of rules which flow from those principles. There are **three principles**, calling on lobbyists to conduct themselves with openness, with integrity and honesty, and in a professional manner. These are, in Wilson's terms, "goals and objectives to be obtained" while the rules set out the "standards" that the principles enjoin. Thus, the principle of openness (or transparency) invokes **three standards**: an obligation to identify to officials the beneficiaries of the lobbying activity and the reasons for it; a commitment to convey information accurately, taking care not to mislead those being lobbied, and, thirdly, a requirement to remind office holders of the lobbyist's own obligation to adhere to the Act and the Code. The standards relating to integrity and honesty are confined to a commitment to respect the confidential nature of information obtained and not to use confidential information "to the disadvantage of their client, employer or organisation". The principle of professionalism is covered by rules relating to "conflict of interest", requiring lobbyists to avoid representing conflicting or competing interests and to avoid placing office holders in positions of conflict of interest.

While these provisions are by no means extensive, they are susceptible to fairly broad interpretation, and can be amended and strengthened. Perhaps more important, the revised Lobbyists Registration Act, in authorising the Code, also conferred on the Registrar powers necessary to **investigate suspected breaches** of the Code, a measure that considerably extended the Registrar's ability to enforce the Lobbyists Registration Act. In addition, the final report of any investigation carried out under the Act must be sent to Parliament. The Registrar has limited authority to take other action on findings that the Act, including the Code has been breached. Prosecution decisions rest with the Attorney General. However, in the lobbying business, where reputation is an important asset, the presentation to Parliament of an authoritative adverse report, and subsequent media interest, can be a significant consequence.[48]

European Commission criteria and rules

As far as codes of conduct are concerned, the central issue that excites debate is not their actual content, but rather their status. **Should they be voluntary? Or enforced with incentives? Or should they be full-fledged regulations?** In its 2006 Green Paper on transparency the European Commission encouraged umbrella organisations of European public affairs practitioners to develop their own codes of conduct using three minimum criteria adopted by the Commission:

- Lobbyists should act in an honest manner and always declare the interest they represent.
- They should not disseminate misleading information.
- They should not offer any form of inducement in order to obtain information or to receive preferential treatment.

The Commission noted with approval that various umbrella organisations had adopted **voluntary** codes based on these standards, and that some have also introduced sanctions such as reprimands and expulsions. Although it reported that only consultant lobbyists are obliged to observe the codes, the Green Paper suggested that European authorities were reluctant to embrace full-fledged imposition and regulation of codes. It invited the profession to develop a code that would cover all lobbyists and that would be part of a voluntary system run by the Commission and made effective through incentives and sanctions (European

Commission, 2006). Whether such a system would secure adequate compliance is a moot point, which can be better taken into consideration after an examination of current procedures for securing compliance.

The Green Paper was opened for public discussion and **consultation** with member states and official bodies during the summer of 2006, and a summary report on the public's views was published in March 2007. This made it clear that neither the general public nor the lobbying community itself shared the Commission's optimism that voluntary participation in a registry or adherence to a code of conduct could be achieved (Commission of the European Union Communities, 2007). The Commission, recognising that self-regulation of lobbying was "not viable", undertook to prepare a draft code of conduct which was discussed with stakeholders in the summer of 2007. It proposed a set of "rules" derived from the principle that:

> Interest representatives are expected to behave in line with the principles of openness, transparency, honesty and integrity, as expected of them by the citizens in a democratic system. The Commission considers that those who register in its public register accept to comply with these principles (European Commission, 2008).

In line with this principle, the Commission approved the Code of Conduct for Interest Representatives[49] that includes **seven basic rules** that representatives should follow. Namely that interest representatives shall always:

- Identify themselves by name and by the entity(ies) they work for or represent.
- Not misrepresent themselves as to the effect of registration to mislead third parties and/or EU staff.
- Declare their interests and, where applicable, the interests of the clients or the members which they represent.
- Ensure that, to the best of their knowledge, the information which they provide is unbiased, complete, up-to date and not misleading.
- Not obtain or try to obtain information or any decision dishonestly.
- Not induce EU staff to contravene rules and standards of behaviour applicable to them.
- If employing former EU staff, respect their obligation to abide by the rules and confidentiality requirements which apply to them.

The Commission remained reluctant to entirely abandon an **incentives approach to registration**, but did propose to create additional incentives. It also proposed additional disclosure requirements, particularly in the area of financial disclosure. On 23 June 2008 the Commission officially launched the Register of Interest Representatives, in just a year, over 1 700 interest representatives were registered.[50] The Commission hopes that eventually a single registry will serve all of the European Union's institutions.

Box 2.7. **Developing the Lobbying Code of Conduct in Australia**

The Australian Government's Lobbying Code of Conduct was released, after public consultation, on 13 May 2008. The aim of the Code is to ensure that lobbying activities are carried out ethically and transparently and that government representatives who are approached by lobbyists are aware of the interests they represent. The Code applies only to "third party" lobbyists, those who lobby professionally on behalf of others. It does not apply to people who directly represent a particular firm or organisation nor does it apply to non-government organisations and charities.

The Code's definition of government representatives covers Australian Public Service (APS) employees and Australian Defence Force personnel as well as ministers and their advisers. Key features of the Code include:

- All professional lobbyists who wish to deal with Government representatives must register with the Department of the Prime Minister and Cabinet. The Register will be available on line and will provide details of the clients and interests the lobbyists represent.
- The Code requires lobbyists not to engage in corrupt, dishonest or illegal activities. It also requires them to inform the Government representatives they approach that they are lobbyists, that they are registered, the name(s) of their clients and the issues they wish to raise. Failure to comply with the Code could mean removal from the Register.
- The Code places restrictions on former Government representatives who wish to work as lobbyists. Former government ministers will not be able to engage in lobbying activities for an 18 month period on any matters on which they have had official dealings as public servants over the last 18 months. Former members of the APS senior executive service will not be able to engage in lobbying activities for a 12 month period on any matters on which they have had official dealings as public servants over the last 12 months.

The Australian Public Service Commission Circular 2008/4 advises agencies of the Code and how it will apply to the APS. It requires agencies to put in place systems to:

- Ensure that staff are aware of the Register and apply the Code in their contacts with lobbyists.
- Enable alleged breaches of the Code to be reported to the Prime Minister and Cabinet.
- Ensure that staff are aware of the post employment restrictions on lobbyists and of their responsibility to ensure, to the best of their ability, that the lobbyists they deal with are not subject to these restrictions.

The Circular also makes it clear that the Code will not affect technical, professional, or programme management contacts or co-operation between the APS and outside companies or organisations.

Securing compliance

Strategies for securing compliance

The imposition of sanctions is often the first recourse of legislators attempting to address issues arising from improper lobbying. **Sanctions are a necessary feature of lobbying legislation, but are seldom sufficiently stringent to constitute a true deterrent.** Even substantial fines or imprisonment, for example, may not intimidate lobbyists who anticipate very large profits from winning significant government contracts for their clients. Again, American experience is a case in point, with the Abramoff scandal being only the most recent example of some lobbyists' irrepressible conviction that it is possible to get away with behaviour that is either illegal or clearly outside the limits of professional conduct. In May 2006, Robert S. Mueller, Director of the FBI revealed that since 9/11 his agency, as part of its increased emphasis on counter-terrorism, had moved more than 200 agents to corruption investigations. By 2004 and 2005:

> More than 1 060 government employees were convicted of corrupt activities, including 177 federal officials, 158 state officials, 360 local officials and 365 police officers, according to FBI statistics. The number of convictions rose 27% from 2004 to 2005 (Johnston, 2006).[51]

Nor is the United States unique. Canada has recently experienced its own "sponsorship scandal" as a result of which a public servant and advertising executives were convicted of colluding over the awarding of contracts. A major public enquiry concluded that **lax enforcement** of regulations, including lobbying regulations, had led to "a culture of entitlement" which permeated government decision making.[52] Tainted by the scandal, the governing Liberals were defeated in the election of January 2005 by the Conservatives, led by Stephen Harper, who made his government's first order of business the introduction of the FAA which has been referred to earlier as strengthening the role of registry officials and tightening disclosure regulations. The political history of many countries contains similar episodes, regardless of the severity of their laws punishing corruption. The United States is endowed with a legislative system in which power is highly diffused and the opportunities for lobbying – legal and illegal – correspondingly abundant. But it is worth remembering that the same openness that encourages lobbying also fosters a competitive advocacy environment and investigative journalism that not only reveals instances of wrong-doing, but creates the impression that America, in comparison to other countries, is riddled with corrupt lobbying practices. Perhaps the United States is more given to spectacular exercises in lobby wrong-doing, but that scarcely means that the rest of the world is free of similar, though less dramatic, activities. The lack of publicity may merely mean that they have not been investigated. As an FBI official wryly commented when the 2004 and 2005 records were revealed, "I don't think anybody recognised the number and quality of cases we would generate".

The lesson of American experience is that sanctions, while important, are only a small part of the regulatory regime that will confine illicit activity to tolerable limits.

One of the obvious concomitants of attempting to limit corrupt practices in lobbying is that sanctions – whether they be fines, imprisonment or denial of access to officials – cannot be imposed unless registry officials are authorised to **require expansions of the information filed** by registrants and accorded the powers of investigation needed to access the tortuous and convoluted trail left by unscrupulous lobbyists. In Canada, for example, early iterations of the Lobbyists Registration Act neglected to give officials sufficient time to identify infractions and carry out investigations. The introduction of the Code of Conduct now enables officials to initiate investigations at any time. This, together with enlargement of powers of investigation has permitted a considerable increase in the number of investigations and, officials believe, greatly enhanced compliance.[53] Enhanced powers, however, do not always lead to successful prosecutions. Registry officials may be required to hand-off investigations once they reveal the possibility of criminal activity. In theory, this is an appropriate demarcation line, one that ensures that eventual prosecution will rest on the findings of investigators experienced in criminal cases. But it may actually result in a failure on the part of the police – who frequently have more urgent priorities – to complete investigations.

These limitations have prompted registry officials to call on legislators to be **more imaginative in developing sanctions that can be applied without criminal prosecutions**. As already noted, the Canadian practice of reporting to Parliament on investigations which have proven violations of the Act conjures up unwelcome publicity for lobbyists. In other jurisdictions, registration constitutes a license to lobby and offences against the regulations, including codes of conduct, can be punished through withdrawal of registration. This approach has been adopted in several European jurisdictions. In Canada, while neither British Columbia, Newfoundland and Quebec, nor the federal government in its new FAA,[54] establish a license system, they do provide for denial of registration. It is unclear whether or not denial would violate rights of Canadian citizens or whether the courts would consider such a sanction too significant for adjudication by an official or even an administrative tribunal.

What is clear, however, is that the **effective use of access as an incentive** to ethical lobbying conduct depends on more than simply issuing or denying passes. As noted, publicity is an important adjunct. So is a system for ensuring that lobbyists who have been denied access, do indeed find doors closed against them at the legislature, the executive and in administrative offices. This can only be achieved if officials and politicians fully understand the nature of the regulatory process and automatically look for evidence that those who lobby them are authorised to do so. It is not enough to enjoin lobbyists to declare their roles and affiliations, or even to insist that they carry authorisation. Those who are lobbied must be able to access registries to verify credentials and they must be expected to carry out verification as a matter of course. This means that there must be managerial directives requiring public servants to verify lobbyists' credentials and to report possible infractions. In turn, the effectiveness of such directives implies that public servants and politicians should be exposed to educational programmes that prepare them to recognise lobbying activity and familiarise them with reporting facilities and requirements.

Education

Compared to the costs of monitoring, investigating and prosecuting lobby wrong-doing, education appears to be **less expensive**.[55] When adequately supported and imaginatively conducted, it can also be far **more effective**. Education strives to create a culture of compliance with the requirements of registration legislation and the ethical standards promulgated by governments. Education programmes address a number of targets. They prepare public officials and lobbyists to understand the role of lobbying in government decision making and to be aware of registration requirements and codes of conduct. The introduction of sessions on lobbying and its regulation can be considered a logical addition to the courses on government ethics that have become a regular part of the curriculum of in-house training programmes. When directed outside government, education can target lobbyists themselves – through their associations, their trade journals, and even, as in the California case, through requiring them to enrol in special training programmes. As for the general public, the academic study of lobbying issues at the university and senior secondary school levels, together with broad outreach to citizen's and business groups, as well as periodic media coverage, helps to create expectations about lobby regulation and public ethics that lobbyists, officials and politicians come to understand must be met. At the same time, they help the public to appreciate the significance and utility of lobbying processes, including knowing how to participate in policy debates, rather than the blanket condemnation of lobbying that is encouraged by sensational coverage of scandals.

In conclusion, it seems evident that compliance is best addressed through a spectrum of strategies that start with clear requirements for inclusive and timely registration and disclosure and go on to include:

- formal sanctions;
- managerial directives requiring public servants to verify lobbyists' credentials and to report possible infractions;

- the endowment of registry officials with adequate powers of investigation and prosecution; and
- education.

Compliance also depends on the development of a culture of integrity throughout governmental institutions. Such a culture reinforces each element of a compliance regime; the lack of a culture of integrity cripples regulation, however carefully devised and expressed it may be. The influence of a regulatory regime and of a culture of integrity will be discussed in a later section.

Government or voluntary regulation?

Earlier reference was made to the suggestion in the European Commission's *Green Paper on the European Transparency Initiative* that the profession be invited to develop a code that would cover all lobbyists and that would be part of a **voluntary system** run by the Commission and made effective through incentives and sanctions (European Commission, 2006). Specifically, the Commission proposed:

- A voluntary registration system, run by the Commission, with clear incentives for lobbyists to register. The incentives would include automatic alerts of consultations on issues of known interest to the lobbyists.
- A common code of conduct for all lobbyists, or at least common minimum requirements. The code should be developed by the lobbying profession itself, possibly consolidating and improving the existing codes.
- A system of monitoring and sanctions to be applied in case of incorrect registration and/or breach of the code of conduct.

A start had been made to implement such a system. According to the Green Paper lobbyists' organisations were encouraged to develop their own codes of conduct based on minima suggested by the Commission. As noted earlier, the resulting **criteria** were:

- Lobbyists should act in an honest manner and always declare the interest they represent.
- They should not disseminate misleading information.
- They should not offer any form of inducement in order to obtain information or receive preferential treatment.

However, as the Green Paper goes on to note, the organisations that signed on to this process represent only a portion of those who lobby in Brussels. Interest group and think-tank employees as well as some members of professional groups, including lawyers, were not covered by these codes (European Commission, 2006). This illustrates the fact that the creation of a **common code depends on securing a shared view of appropriate conduct** in this domain on the part of different professional bodies. Public relations specialists, journalists, lawyers, managers, accountants and even doctors and engineers can be found in the world of lobbying. Most of these fields are represented by professional bodies that have widely varying capacities to discipline their members and diverse views on what constitutes appropriate conduct. The later proposed draft Code of Conduct for Interest Representatives implicitly acknowledged the difficulty of securing agreement on a code amongst so many groups when it broadly defined "interest representation" as "the activities carried out with the objective of influencing the policy formulation and decision-making processes of the European institutions" (European Commission, 2008).

Assuming that this definition makes it possible to arrive at a Code that covers most of those who lobby in Brussels, the question arises as to whether the proposed incentives will be sufficient to encourage lobbyists to observe the Code. In the North American context the promise of "automatic alerts of consultations on issues of known interest to the lobbyists" would be insufficient. Lobbyists, after all, are in the business of "knowing what is going on". A somewhat **more stringent incentive** in some European jurisdictions is the practice of making registration a prerequisite to participation in consultations. This would be a more powerful incentive than simple notification, as long as formal participation was necessary to the lobbyists involved. It would not be an incentive for those lobbyists who use less formal means for influencing legislators and officials. On the other hand, if the theatre of lobbying activity were to be broadly defined, as suggested earlier, and if the privilege of access were to be dependent on strict observance of the Code, there might be sufficient incentive to bring the majority of lobbyists into compliance.

This brings us to the last of the Commission's proposals. **Monitoring compliance** is most likely to be achieved on a systematic and comprehensive basis if it is carried out by officials, and if those officials have authority to investigate non-compliance. And while some assistance in monitoring can be expected from members of the public, the media and lobbyists themselves, the most consistent source of information about lobbying activity has to be public officials. The people who are being lobbied are in the best position to require lobbyists to observe ethics codes and to report failures to do so. Their effectiveness, however, will depend on the extent to which they are familiar with the regulations regarding lobbying and with their own obligation to assist the monitoring process.

This last point suggests that while it may be possible to mount a lobby registration scheme on a voluntary basis, in the final analysis its success will depend on a **level of enforcement that can only be achieved at the governmental level**. Only government has the authority to require lobbyists to divulge information. Only government can require officials to report the failure of lobbyists to comply with the rules. Only government can investigate such failures and prosecute breaches of the rules. Only government can impose sanctions such as the denial of access.

Perhaps the achievement of a **culture of integrity**, such as was alluded to at the conclusion of our discussion of sanctions and compliance, would obviate the need for coercive measures and permit dependence on voluntary conformity with codes of conduct established by professional bodies. Canada's experience in the sponsorship scandal – which revealed that a number of lobbyists had not troubled to register – demonstrates that, in this country at least, no such culture exists, and some degree of coercion is necessary. It may be that a combination of governmental and voluntary arrangements, such as has been suggested for Brussels, can be made to work, but, again the Canadian experience suggests otherwise. In the several reviews that have been conducted of the lobbying legislation, lobbyist organisations have argued against measures that would introduce greater transparency. The Canadian code was developed in consultation with lobbyists, and can be hardly considered rigorous; quite possibly a code that was entirely a product produced by lobbyists themselves would be even more permissive.

Several arguments have been put in favour of a **voluntary approach**. The *Sixth Report of the British House of Commons Committee on Standards in Public Life* concluded that "the weight of evidence is against regulation by means of a compulsory register and code of conduct". The evidence cited by the Committee warrants comment.

First, the Committee felt that "the credibility of compulsory regulation schemes is often diminished by amendments to the rules. An elaborate, frequently changing system could produce unfairness, evasion and bureaucratic complexity". The evidence supporting this view was "the history in the United States, Canada and Australia in particular, of amendments to regulatory schemes to fill a succession of loopholes". Whether the Australian registry was in existence long enough to experience elaborate and frequently changing rules, is questionable, but it is true that Canada and the United States have discussed a number of schemes to fill loopholes, and changes have been introduced. Doubtless these processes have created problems for lobbying firms,[56] but revisions of regulations are only to be expected when, as in the Canadian case, the **state enters a new field**. While the leaders of different governments may want to achieve similar objectives, such as transparency and integrity in public policy making, the political cultures and constitutional arrangements of their respective countries force each government that begins lobby regulation to invent its own approach. There is, as already argued, no "boiler-plate" legislation available. Even in the United States, where lobby regulation has been attempted for over a century, changes in public attitudes, in the scale of government activity, in the processes of party politics and public decision making, as well as in the technologies of political communication have all fostered a continuing debate over regulation. Both countries have been going through, and will continue to go through, a period of political learning in this field. It is doubtful that the adoption of a voluntary approach would have avoided this evolution.

The second criticism is that defining lobbyists and lobbying, and distinguishing the latter "from the simple provision of information would be difficult"; a point also made in the present discussion. Nevertheless, as the discussion also demonstrates, **definitions have been achieved** by North American governments, and probably as effectively as in more voluntary systems. Indeed, the assertion in the Sixth Report that "the self-regulation schemes operated by lobbyists" organisations are already moving toward greater convergence', suggests that differences in approach and practice have been a problem. The fact that some of these groups have themselves recommended government take a lead in regulation suggests that harmonisation is more difficult to achieve than the Committee would have us believe.

An argument that may have carried more weight with the Committee than these stems from the very advice given by the professional lobby groups. Namely, that by creating a "category of 'registered' or 'licensed' lobbyist" government would "give the impression that access to government could only be gained through the employment of that kind of company". In support of this view, the Committee quoted Justin Greenwood to the effect that:

> Those schemes which are based on a declaration of clients by lobby firms tend to benefit lobby firms seeking intelligence on their competitors at the public expense. While lobbyists are no doubt concerned to improve standards, they tend to seek regulation to enhance their own status by controlling access to the profession and by seeking recognition (Sixth Report, p. 87).

Some of the consequences of lobby registration may be pernicious in the manner Professor Greenwood suggests. Competition between firms, as a result of lobbyists' trolling for business, can complicate decision processes and increase the costs of public administration. But not all the lobbyists who watch the registers are business competitors; some are employees of **public interest groups**, such as Democracy Watch, in Canada, and Common Cause (and a host of others) in the United States. Their intervention, while irritating to many consultant lobbyists, is frequently in the public interest. Nor is it appropriate to dismiss the registers because only lobbyists and journalists follow them. The lobbying field is a specialised one in journalism as it is in business, and those journalists who regularly follow the registers play an important role in disseminating information about lobbying to their colleagues and to the public at large.[57] Finally, it has to be remembered that one of the objectives behind the creation of registers is **efficacy**. It is helpful to government officials to know who the lobbyists are, who they represent, what they are trying achieve and, if possible, how they are trying to achieve it. To some extent use of the registries depends on education and familiarity with the data available. In 2005-06, the website for the Canadian Federal Registry recorded 82 230 visits (a 96% annual increase in the number of hits), following a period of heightened public interest in lobbying issues, the beginnings of an education programme mounted by the Registry and stricter monitoring and verification by Registry officials. Does a registration system create two-tier access to government as the British Committee suggests? The Committee cites a number of British charities, as well as Professor Greenwood, to this effect. On the other hand, it is doubtful that the creation of the lobbyist registration process in Canada, or its counterpart in the United States, has done anything more than reveal a situation that has existed for many years. A two-tiered system exists because of the growing complexity of government, and the need for guidance in understanding and approaching decision centres. The present author has interviewed a number of directors of Canadian charities about their activities in public policy development. These individuals referred to the Lobbyist Registration Act as adding to the paper burden that they have to carry, but **none suggested that registration has made it more difficult for them to gain access to decision makers**. Some commented that it has helped them to track the activities of lobbyists working for interests that they oppose.

Arguments for formal regulation seem more compelling than those against, as presented in the Sixth Report. As will be argued shortly, registration schemes address fundamental issues associated with applying the principles of open government and of working towards integrity in government. At a more mundane level, governments are in a better position than lobbyists' organisations to work towards standard rules for lobbying and to provide both lobbyists and the public with reliable data about them and their activities. Again, Canadian experience confirms one of the positive observations of the British Committee: that registration does encourage lobbyist organisations to deal with ethical issues and to improve the standing of practitioners in the eyes of the public. But most important, governments possess the authority to insist that lobbyists, on pain of losing either reputation, access, or, in the worst cases, freedom, conform to certain standards of behaviour. Professional organisations, even with government encouragement, find it difficult to effectively discipline their members. As Canadian and American experience attests, enforcement of standards has not been easy for government either, but **over the long run, as regulatory systems develop, governments stand a better chance than professional organisations of securing compliance with regulations**.

The place of lobby regulation in the regulatory regime

Where lobbying legislation is in place, it is one of a group of laws, policies and practices that define the quality of governance in the state. Taken together, they can be termed a regulatory regime. Even more than lobby regulation, these laws will **reflect the national context** in which they are developed, and so are far from being identical from one country to another. Nevertheless, common elements can be found. Among the more important of these, particularly from the perspective of lobby regulation, are laws, policies and practices which regulate the legislature and its members; govern the internal management, including the financial management, of the public service; provide for oversight of the executive by independent agencies appointed by the legislature; regulate elections; codify the criminal law, and define the relationships between citizens and the state.

The principal significance of this regulatory regime is that it establishes the **culture of government**. It is through this regime, that public aspirations for transparency, integrity and efficacy are authoritatively expressed. Interdependent, mutually reinforcing, the constituent elements of the regulatory regime create the environment that fosters – or discourages – the attainment of these aspirations.

Although all elements of the regime can influence lobby regulation, the influence of some is more important than that of others. Their significance, too, will vary from one country to another. In most jurisdictions, the regulation of the legislature itself and of the conduct of legislators and officials of government are extremely important. As already explained, these rules vary from legislature to legislature, and that variation affects the relationship between legislatures and the representatives of interests. In some legislatures "dual mandates" are a matter of course; in others, they are a criminal offence. Even so, in many countries there is a growing concern to monitor, and often to regulate, the behaviour of legislators and officials both while they serve and for specific periods after service. It is increasingly realised that **public officials have access to knowledge and to other office holders that is a commodity in the lobbyist's world**; a commodity whose purchase provides an unfair advantage to the lobbyist's clients (Kirkpatrick, 2006).[58]

Financial management policies

Financial management policies are also significant factors in lobby regulation. Advertised calls for bids, competitive bidding, project evaluation, and bans on contingency fees all constitute a framework that is supposed to govern the behaviour of lobbyists when they **represent clients seeking government contracts**. Failure to conform with financial management legislation, regulations and policy guidelines may be detected through audits conducted by oversight authorities and can lead to prosecution under criminal law. Thus the lobbying framework created by financial management polices is reinforced by oversight legislation and the criminal law.

In most states, but particularly in North America, election law is closely tied to lobby regulation. Historically lobbyists and their clients have found that campaign finance is a sure route to the warm regard of legislators. As one Canadian businessman argued, you have to give money to politicians to get their help:

> I prefer to do that [give to politician's election campaigns] than start running around after the election saying there was a misunderstanding. Then you risk being misunderstood for four years. The risk is big. In business, we sometimes need the help of bureaucrats and MPs (*Toronto Globe and Mail*, 1999, p. A4).

Lobby regulation plays a modest role in this regime, but it can be a key strand in the web. In Canada, for example, it would be hard to identify the extent of the "revolving door" problem, and so hard to know whether or not the Values and Ethics Code for the Public Service is accomplishing its purpose, were it not for the disclosure provisions of lobbying legislation. Without it, as well, major contributors to, and important officials of political parties, would not be identified as lobbyists, so that it would be hard to establish a connection between the operations of political parties and the exercise of influence. The Lobbying Act, as the Lobbyists Registration Act is now called, and elections legislation thus work together to shed light on what has been a murky part of Canadian public life. Again, the provisions of the Act have helped to operationalise Treasury Board rules regarding the letting of contracts, identifying, for example, instances in which lobbyists may have received contingency fees for their assistance in obtaining contracts, contrary to Treasury Board rules.

European Transparency Initiative and Green Paper

The significance of the regulatory regime becomes strikingly apparent when the goals that the European Community has set for its institutions at Brussels are considered. In the words of the 2006 Green Paper:

> The Commission believes that high standards of transparency are part of the legitimacy of any modern administration. The European public is entitled to expect efficient, accountable and service-minded public institutions and that the power and resources entrusted to political and public bodies are handled with care and never abused for personal gain (European Commission, 2006).

The principles of transparency, integrity and efficacy are here laid out. The Green Paper goes on to demonstrate the role a regulatory regime plays in realising these principles. Access to documents legislation, the creation of publicly accessible data bases relating to public consultation, the enhancement of codes of conduct for legislators and officials and the establishment of policies and routines for evaluating and publicly reviewing policy proposals have all been part of the **move toward transparency**. The Green Paper:

> With the European Transparency Initiative, the Commission has launched a review of its overall approach to transparency. The aim is to identify and stimulate a debate on areas for improvement. Consequently, the Initiative covers a broad spectrum of issues. These range from fuller information about management and use of Community funds to professional ethics in the European institutions and the framework in which lobby groups and civil society organisations are operating (European Commission, 2006).

It illustrates how the decision to accept specific principles of governance introduces a **compelling logic into a variety of regulatory areas** that changes every component as each is made compatible with the core principles and restructured to create an interdependent regime. In this transformation, lobby regulation is itself changed. To reflect, for example, the Commission's commitment that "relations between the Commission and interest representatives must be open to outside scrutiny" (European Commission, 2006), lobby regulation is strengthened and acquires heightened significance. At the same time, however, the dependence of lobby regulation on the other elements of the regime becomes apparent, requiring, as the European developments illustrate, appropriate revisions of other statutes, policies and practices.

In sum, **lobby regulation can neither be initiated nor reformed in isolation**. As part of a complex regulatory regime, it must affect, and be affected by, other elements of the regime. Accordingly, its creation or modification must be synchronised with the revision of those other elements.

Establishing and maintaining the integrity of the regulatory regime

The history of lobby regulation is one of the periods of inaction interspersed with spasms of reform triggered by scandal. The periods of inaction are not devoid of development or without significance. On the contrary, the routine application – or, as in many cases, lack of application – of the regulations reveals their strengths and weaknesses. Occasions arise for public comment and discussion of suggestions for reform. These discussions prepare the way for the changes that seem to come so suddenly in the aftermath of scandal.

Evolution of institutional framework for implementing federal lobby regulations in the United States and Canada

This has been the pattern of development for Canada's federal lobby regulations. It became clear before the first Lobbyists Registration Act was passed that it was a weak piece of legislation, and that the administration of the Act would be influenced by the wishes of the government of the day. This proved to be the case.

A central problem was that the Registrar of Lobbyists was a civil servant and that the Office was located in the executive part of government. The Registrar, who was not a senior official, was consequently ultimately subject to the pressures that ministers and other senior officials could bring to bear. It was absurd to expect this official to interview Ministers of the Crown in order to determine whether infringements of the Act, or the Code of Conduct, had taken place. Yet this was what the Act ordained. Furthermore, the Office was **vulnerable to budgetary, staffing and organisational decisions** that severely limited its effectiveness.

One of the saving graces of the early version of the Act was a clause that required a committee of Parliament to review its administration and operation on the third year after the Act's coming into force (Section 14). Several reviews have taken place, and **each has led to significant improvements** in the Act. Each also saw the raising of issues that were not addressed and that did not lead to change, but that did influence subsequent reviews.

Amongst the most contentious of these was the suggestion that the Lobbyists Registration Branch should be removed from its place in a line department and put under the supervision of Parliament itself. This proposal was put forward in 1993 at the first review, and repeated in subsequent reviews. The argument was straightforward: the Registrar and the Branch, located as they were in a line department, were **exposed to improper influence**. Such influence would be reduced if the Registrar was made an Officer of Parliament and his/her appointment protected.

The argument was dismissed by successive review committees, dominated as they were by members on the government side, but the status of the Registrar was enhanced and the powers of the office were strengthened. Eventually, however, in the aftermath of the sponsorship scandal, the proposal was endorsed by the Commission of Enquiry and found its way into the election platform of the Conservative Party, which, on coming to power, lost no time in introducing the FAA. Section 68 provides that the government of the day shall consult with the leaders of all other Parliamentary parties before appointing a Commissioner of Lobbyists, and that the appointment should be approved by resolution of both Houses of Parliament. The Commissioner shall hold office for seven years, though subject to removal for cause through an address of both Houses.

It is too early to evaluate this reform, but in theory the Commissioner should be in a position to **exercise his or her responsibilities without fear or favour**. Above all, the great advantage of appointment and regulation by Parliament lies in the fact that the legislature itself is an open forum. It is a centre of media attention, and it has an authority that cannot be gained at all easily by agencies in the executive branch. Notwithstanding any proclivity individual members may have for secrecy or for protecting the perquisites of their party organisations, the competitive nature of the House and its underlying responsibility for the public interest, will in the long run support an agency that is charged with promoting transparency and genuinely enabling "public office holders and the public... to know who is attempting to influence government". Furthermore, even though the administration of the Registry is subject to the rules of the public service, the fact that the Commissioner can obtain the ear of Parliament suggests that in matters of staffing and management the Registry will have resources to match its responsibilities.

The rationale for these reforms is that the **autonomy** of the Commissioner of Lobbyists is essential to ensuring the continued integrity of lobby regulation. In the Canadian case this has certainly been true of Auditors General, who carry out their responsibilities in a similar way. In other jurisdictions, comparable levels of autonomy have proven their worth. It is the case with the Quebec Commissioner of Lobbyists and at least two American states, New York and New Jersey. It is noteworthy that, following a long campaign led by Representative Nancy Pelosi, the Speaker of the US House of Representatives (Weisman and Birnbaum, 2007), the Congress passed the Honest Leadership and Open Government Act of 2007 and the Office of Congressional Ethics was created to investigate "suspect wrongdoing by lawmakers". This measure moves oversight of House ethics toward greater autonomy, as the Office panel will consist of six people of "exceptional public standing" who are not members of the House. It is expected to effect a major improvement in the enforcement of ethics rules (Hurse, 2008).

Even though experience suggests that **autonomy holds considerable promise, it is not without risk**. A great deal depends on the quality of the individuals recommended to lead the regulatory agency. Governments able to command a majority in the legislature could impose a weak candidate. Furthermore, legislators themselves have often proven unwilling to accept levels of regulation that they have promoted on the hustings. It is possible that their collective sense of self-preservation would at times constrain the gathering of information and the carrying out of investigations. Too, parliamentary bodies have shown themselves capable of limiting resources and clipping mandates. Nevertheless, the likelihood of these risks occurring under a parliamentary regime is far less than it would be were the regulatory programmes to be housed in line departments.

A concomitant necessity is that the goal of transparency should be paramount in the management and reporting arrangements of the registry. In the US and Canada the fact that the registries are publicly available has meant that the media, and interests themselves, have **confirmed their utility**, while the fact that reports into confirmed violations of the regulations are presented to Parliament and made public is a substantial incentive for compliance. No lobbyist who plans to remain in business wants to be known, like Jack Abramoff, as "the disgraced lobbyist".[59] The most important asset of any lobbyist is his or her capacity to access decision makers. Public officials, elected and unelected, are distinctly unwilling to consort with lobbyists with dubious reputations.

On balance, experience in the United States, Australia and Canada affirms that to be effective lobby regulation must be overseen by an official of high standing appointed by the legislature, independent of the government of the day for a fixed term and otherwise removable only through a formal legislative process.

Notes

1. This chapter was prepared by Professor A.P. Pross, Professor Emeritus in the School of Public Administration, Dalhousie University, Halifax, Nova Scotia, Canada. The author wishes to acknowledge the kind assistance of Michael Nelson, Canada's Registrar of Lobbyists, Mr. André C. Côté, *Commissaire au lobbyisme du Québec*, Kerry MacLean, Director, Strategy and Innovation Division, Service Nova Scotia, André Ouimet, *Directeur des services juridiques, Commissaire au lobbyisme du Québec*, and János Bertók, Principal Administrator, Innovation and Integrity Division of the OECD Public Governance and Territorial Development Directorate. The author would also like to thank the Council on Government Ethics Laws (COGEL) for providing information.
2. Lobbyists are also described in terms familiar in pluralist systems.
3. The Bureau has the power to implement the decisions of the National Assembly and to organise and supervise its services and activities (Article 14 of the Constitution). The Bureau is composed of 22 members including the President of the Assembly and the six vice-presidents.
4. *www.assemblee-nationale.fr/representants-interets/fiche_renseignements.pdf.*
5. The *Code de conduite applicable aux représentants d'intérêts*, was adopted by the Bureau on 2 July 2009, *www.assemblee-nationale.fr/representants-interets/index.asp#code.*
6. The first US federal exercise in lobby regulation followed this pattern. In 1876, the US House of Representatives adopted a resolution requiring lobbyists to register with the Clerk of the House. The resolution had effect only for the duration of the 44th Congress. This was also the pattern at the Canadian federal level, where the first Lobbyists Registration Act emphasised transparency, through monitoring lobbying activity, On the other hand, several US state legislatures moved immediately to stringent regulation. Between 1873 and 1905 Alabama, Georgia, California and Wisconsin declared lobbying a felony.

7. As lobbyists registration acts evolve they may explicitly affirm provisions that are to be found elsewhere. For example, Quebec's act invokes a two-year moratorium on cabinet members and senior municipals lobbying the governments or institutions with which they were previously associated and a one-year moratorium on former senior public office servants. R.S.Q. Chapter T 11.011, Section 29 and Section 30.
8. This is a continuing issue in Britain where convention has permitted Parliamentarians to accept consultancies, and in Germany where the "Provisions for the Rules of Conduct for the Members of the *Bundestag*" (1972) recognise that members often represent specific organisations.
9. Canada, House of Commons, Bill C-2 An Act providing for conflict of interest rules, restrictions on election financing and measures respecting administrative transparency, oversight and accountability 55 Eliz. II, 2006 (as passed by the Commons, June 21, 2006). At the time of writing, the Act has been assented to but not brought into effect. It is consequently difficult to access on the web. The Royal Assent version can be found, at this time, at *www.parl.gc.ca/LEGININFO/index.asp?Language=E&Chamber=N&StartList=A&EndList=Z&Session=14&Type=0&Scope=I&query=4649&List=toc-1*. The Act illustrates the point being made here: It is omnibus legislation folding together measures relating to lobbying, ethics, election financing, whistle-blowing and Parliamentary monitoring of government expenditure. Included in the Bill are extensive amendments to the Lobbyists Registration Act (renamed the Lobbying Act) which, in contrast to earlier lobbying legislation, regulate the post-employment behaviour of senior officials. For example, Section 75 of the Bill prohibits senior public office holders from engaging in paid lobbying activities. Earlier versions of the Lobbyists Registration Act simply required registrants to disclose whether the lobbyist had been a public office holder and which offices had been held. The actual post-employment prohibition on lobbying activity was to be found in the ethics codes for public office holders and civil servants. See Office of the Ethics Commissioner, Conflict of Interest Code and Post-Employment Code for Public Office Holders, Section 28, and Treasury Board of Canada Secretariat, Values and Ethics Code for the Public Service, Chapter 3. The new rules considerably extend the moratorium period for senior public office holders.
10. For somewhat different reasons – chiefly a desire to avoid administrative bottlenecks for both public and officials – routine administrative communications are not considered to be lobbying activities.
11. Greenwood suggests that decisions to regulate lobbyists are precipitated by one or other of these considerations, and most frequently by the need to address issues arising from scandals. All three factors may be at play. In Canada, for example, private members attempted on a number of occasions at the federal level to introduce legislation regulating lobbying, because, as they said, they were concerned in broad terms about public perceptions of government and access. Their efforts bore fruit in 1985 when the Mulroney government undertook to include lobby regulation in an ethics package that had been promised in the previous election and may have been brought forward by Prime Minister Mulroney following some early charges levelled against his administration.
12. However, in late 2006 the State of Western Australia established a code of conduct for contact between lobbyists and officials and created a lobbyists register. The enabling legislation is the State's Public Sector Management Act of 1994, *www.lobbyregister.dpc.wa.gov.au*.
13. During the public hearings of Canada's Commission of Inquiry into the Sponsorship Program and Advertising Activities, many witnesses revealed that they had not registered, that the Commissioner commented wryly that he had

"the impression that nobody registers as a lobbyist. … I haven't heard (of) one case so far" (Commission of Inquiry into the Sponsorship Program and Advertising Activities Public Hearing [Translation], Vol. 110, p. 20193). One witness, Alain Renaud, explained that "I didn't do it because it was standard practice. In the communications field, most people were not registered. So I was not alone" (Public Hearing [Translation], Vol. 96. p. 17136).

14. Lobbyists Registration Act (2004), Section 5. The informal version of the current Act will be found at the website of the Office of the Registrar of Lobbyists (*http://strategis.is.gc.ca/epic/internet/inlobbyist-lobbyiste.nsf/en/nx00101e.html*). The present Act is a consolidation of the Lobbyists Registration Act, R.S. 1985, Chapter 44 (4th Supp.); An Act to Amend the Lobbyists Registration Act and to make related amendments to other Acts, S.C 1995, Chapter 12; 25 July 1995, January 31, 1996 and the remainder from Bill C-15 on June 11, 2003; and An Act to amend the Parliament of Canada Act (Ethics Commissioner and Senate Ethics Officer) and other Acts in consequence, Bill C-4, which came into force on 17 May 2004.

15. Letter, Diane Champagne-Paul, Registrar, Lobbyists Registration, to Richard Dupuis, Clerk, House of Commons Standing Committee on Industry Science and Technology, 30 April 2001.

16. Telephone interview with André Côté, Commissioner of Lobbyists, Quebec, 22 January 2007.

17. For example, Ontario's Lobbyists Registration Act, Chapter 27, Ontario Statutes, 1998, Section 3 (1) provides that the Act "does not apply to the following persons when acting in their official capacity: (4) Members of the council of a band as defined in Subsection 2 (1) of the Indian Act (Canada) or of the council of an Indian band established by an Act of the Parliament of Canada, persons on the staff of these members or employees of the council".

18. An Act to Amend the Parliament of Canada Act (Ethics Commissioner and Senate Ethics Officer) and other Acts in consequence Bill C-4. In effect 17 May 2004. Section 4.2.c.

19. "An Act to Amend the Parliament of Canada Act (Ethics Commissioner and Senate Ethics Officer) and other Acts in consequence Bill C-4. In effect 17 May 2004. Section 5.2.f provides that the registrant must "identify any communication techniques, including appeals to members of the public through the mass media or by direct communication that seek to persuade members of the public to communicate directly with a public office holder in an attempt to place pressure on the public office holder to endorse a particular opinion (in this Act referred to as 'grass-roots communication'), that the individual has used or expects to use in an attempt to influence that matter." An interesting feature of American regulation is that while the Lobbying Disclosure Act does not compel lobbyists to report grass-roots activities, the Internal Revenue Code (Section 4911) imposes a tax on expenditures exceeding certain amounts, and thereby forces organisations to report they have spent on grass-roots lobbying. See US General Accounting Office, "Federal Lobbying: Differences in Lobbying Definitions and their Impact", Washington DC, GAO/GGD-99-38.

20. *www.com2006_0194_en.pdf*.

21. John Chenier, editor of *The Lobby Monitor* noted in testimony before the House of Commons Standing Committee on Industry, Science, and Technology that recent US state legislation has begun to include "a component to identify the expenditures involved in lobby campaigns in order to provide some measure of (the) intensity of the campaign, as well as who is involved" (Proceedings and Evidence, 24 April 2005).

The Monitor frequently cites US data on lobbying activity. Its October, 2003, issue commented on a study by the Annenburg Public Policy Center at the University of Pennsylvania which looked at lobby advertising. It reported that in 2001 and 2002 lobbies spent USD 105 million in the Washington DC area alone on advertising relating to issues before the President and Congress. Eleven organisations spent 40% of this amount. In addition to drawing attention to the big spenders, the study found a correlation between heavy spending on advertising and policy success. It warned that "organisations that are spending large amounts regularly to influence public policy may be of greater concern than the occasional large spender because this could indicate that a small sector of the public is consistently having more influence on issues of public policy".

22. This issue, like the argument that public interest groups are discriminated against by the LRA, impinges on a concern that has troubled supporters of public interest groups for a number of years. That is, that commercial enterprises can treat the costs of lobbying as legitimate business expenses. Since such expenses reduce corporate taxes, the public is, in effect, paying part of the costs of lobbying its own government. This is offensive to public interest groups on several grounds. First, such groups are themselves required to report such sums as they receive from government. Second, charities – which constitute a large proportion of Canada's active public interest groups – face strict regulations governing their expenditure on lobbying. However, worthy their cause, no one charity can spend more than 10% of its annual income on lobbying. Furthermore, there are even stricter regulations prohibiting politically partisan advocacy and some forms of policy advocacy. Third, corporations' capacity to raise funds for lobbying far exceeds that of public interest groups. Many such groups have registered as charities because the tax incentive for charitable donations does encourage donations. Those that have determined to remain as non-profit organisations in order to avoid the advocacy restrictions applied to charities find that public financial support is quite limited. In short, neither group has the resources, or in many cases is permitted, to challenge corporate lobbying on anything like equal terms.

23. US GAO Differences in Lobbying Definitions, Washington DC: Report to Congressional Committees, GAO/GGD-99-38), pp. 2-3. The official Guide to the Lobbying Disclosure Act issued by the Office of the Clerk of the House of Representatives notes that "the tax definition of lobbying is broader with respect to the type of activities reported, while they are narrower with respect to executive branch officials contacted" (*http://lobbyingdisclosure.house.gov/lda_guide.html*, p. 9 "Lobbying contacts and activities using Section 15 election").

24. The Executive Order includes ban on accepting gifts from registered lobbyists or lobbying organisations, *www.whitehouse.gov/issues/ethics*.

25. The cost estimate was given in the Canaday Report, p. 12. The estimates of Washington lobbyists' earnings will be found in Robert G. Kaiser, "The Power Player", *Washington Post*, 3 March 2007.

26. Center for Responsive Politics, Lobbying Database can be consulted at *www.opensecrets.org/lobby/index.php*.

27. The Center for Public Integrity gathered overall, aggregate spending totals available in 43 states for 2006. Collected data on state lobbying can be consulted at *http://projects.publicintegrity.org/hiredguns/chart.aspx?act=lobbyspending*.

28. Standing Committee on Elections, Privileges and Procedure. "First Report to the House", Minutes of Proceedings and Evidence1/33, 1985-86, 12:4-10.

29. Letter, D.A. Greekie, director, Department of Communications and Government Relations. Canadian Medical Association. to Albert Cooper, Chairman, Standing Committee on Elections, Privileges and Procedure, 28 April 1986. See also the testimony by Donald Thom, Standing Committee, Proceedings, 11:30.

30. The battle over tobacco regulation assumed similar proportions in most countries. The American version can be found in Devra Davies *The Secret History of the War on Cancer* (NY: Basic Books, 2007) and the Canadian in R. Cunningham, *Smoke and Mirrors: The Canadian Tobacco War* (Ottawa: International Development Research Centre, 1996). A shorter discussion which concentrates on the lobbying aspects of the health lobby campaign can be found in A. Paul Pross and Iain S. Stewart, "Breaking the Habit: Attentive Publics and Tobacco Regulation", in S.D. Phillips (ed.), *How Ottawa Spends, 1994-95: Making Change*, Ottawa: Carleton University Press, 1994, pp.129-165.

31. Section 9 (9), Corporations and other organisations are not required to report comparable information. The zones are: less than CAD 10 000; CAD 10-50 000; CAD 50 000 to CAD 100 000, and over CAD 100 000.

32. Telephone interview, 7 December 2006.

33. This point is frequently made by Canadian observers, particularly by the editor of *The Lobby Monitor* whose newsletter is widely read in the lobbying community. Professor Justin Greenwood, in his testimony to the United Kingdom House of Commons Committee on Standards argued that "those schemes which are based on a declaration of clients by lobby firms tend to benefit lobby firms seeking intelligence on their competitors at the public expense", Sixth Report, p. 87.

34. Lobbyist Registration Branch. A Guide to Registration as of 26 August 2005 at *http://strategis.ic.gc.ca/epic/internet/inlobbyist-lobbyiste.nsf/en/nx00112e.html*.

35. As, for example, in Germany. See European Commission, *Green Paper on the European Transparency Initiative*, p. 7.

36. These examples have been drawn from a recent issue of *The Lobby Monitor*.

37. A "covered executive branch official" includes the President, the Vice-President and other officials specified by their civil service or military grade and "serving in a position of a confidential, policy-determining, policy making, or policy-advocating character" described in Section 7511 (b) (2) of Title 5 United States Code. A similar list of members of congress and employees in that branch describes "covered legislative branch officials".

38. Alberta Legislative Assembly 3rd Session 26th Legislature, 2007, Bill 1 "Lobbyists Act" Section 3 (2)[c] exempts communications to public office holders "in response to a request initiated by a public office holder for advice or comment" on legislative proposals, development of regulations, etc. The Federal Lobbyists Registration Act on the other hand exempts similar communications only if the request initiated by the public office holder is "restricted to a request for information".

39. United Kingdom, House of Commons, Sixth Report of the Committee on Standards, p. 84, quoting the "Appendix to the Nineteenth Report of the House of Commons Select Committee on Standards and Privileges", [HC 1147 (1997-98)], p. v.

40. The Register became fully operational from 1 July 2008, *http://lobbyists.pmc.gov.au/lobbyistsregister/index.cfm*.

41. According to the Annual Reports of the Canadian Registrar, 99% of registrations are submitted over the Internet.

42. At this time, in Washington, they must give more detailed information about the issue areas they are lobbying in – listing specific areas, bill numbers and executive actions; the legislative branches or executive agencies contact, and the income received or expenses incurred. "The Lobbying Disclosure Act of 1995", Section 5. Canadian laws, in addition to semi-annual updates, require immediate reporting of significant changes in lobby undertakings. See, for example, the *Guide to the Nova Scotia Registry of Lobbyists*.

43. The Sixth Report cites the case of two firms that were suspended from membership in the Association of Professional Political Consultants following an inquiry. The internal arrangements of the firms were investigated by third parties and the firms eventually reinstated (p. 85).

44. "Rules of Procedure of the European Parliament". Annex IX "Provisions governing the application of Rule 9(2) – Lobbying in the European Parliament", Article 3 "Code of Conduct", (f).

45. Such as obtaining information dishonestly, claiming any formal relationship with the Parliament in dealings with other, and circulating, for profit, copies of documents obtained from Parliament. Article 3, Sections (b) to (e).

46. The amendments that came into effect in May 2004 transferred responsibility for the Code to the Registrar.

47. Newfoundland, Lobbyists Registration Act SNL 2004 Chapter L 24.1, Section 25 and the Quebec Lobbying Transparency and Ethics Act, Sections 36-38.

48. The filing before Parliament of an adverse report is clearly a more momentous event than the advertising of disciplinary action by a professional body, but to date there is very little concrete evidence of whether or not critical publicity in either venue actually results in a loss of business.

49. *https://webgate.ec.europa.eu/transparency/regrin/infos/codeofconduct.do?locale=en#en.*

50. On 31 July 2009 there were 1 756 interest representatives in the register, see *https://webgate.ec.europa.eu/transparency/regrin/consultation/statistics.do#.*

51. The Internal Revenue Service, which monitors charities, has also found, despite increasingly restrictive campaign finance laws, "a disturbing amount of political intervention in charities in the last election cycle", including "a staggering increase in money flowing (illegally) into campaigns". "RS finds sharp increase in illegal political activity", *New York Times*, 25 February 2006.

52. Commission of Inquiry into the Sponsorship Program and Advertising Activities. Reports, Ottawa, 2005 and 2006. A review, by the present author, of "The Lobbyists Registration Act, its Application and Effectiveness" will be found in the Commission's research studies: *Restoring Accountability: Research Studies*, Ottawa, 2006, Vol. 2, pp. 163-231.

53. Between 2004 and 2006 the Canadian registry has been extensively reorganised and expanded. Additional staff has been hired, permitting closer monitoring of registrations and follow-up enquiries. More investigations have also been carried out. In 2005-6 6 994 registrations were processed. The previous year 1 638 registrations were processed (see Office of the Registrar of Lobbyists). Lobbyists Registration Act. Annual Reports for the respective years. Data will be found in the "Statistical Review" section.

54. See British Columbia, Office of the Registrar, *A Guide to the Lobbyists Registration Act*, Victoria: The Office, July 2003, p. 5; Statutes of Newfoundland and Labrador 2004 Chapter L-24.1 Lobbyists Registration Act, Section 28 (1); Quebec Lobbying

Transparency and Ethics Act, ss. 25 and 53., and the Federal Accountability Act, Section 80. 14.01.

55. The "Management Representation Statement" contained in the 2006-07 Report on Plans and Priorities (RPP) for the Office of the Registrar of Lobbyists states that the Office's education programme, through which the Office "develops and implements educational and research programmes to foster awareness of the requirements of the Lobbyists Registration Act and the Lobbyists' Code of Conduct" is scheduled to cost CAD 909 000 in each of the current and next budget year. Most of this programme will be directed to lobbyists, their clients and public office holders. Reviews and Investigations under the Lobbyists Registration Act and the Lobbyists' Code of Conduct will cost CAD 1 050 000 in each of those two years. It will involve validating information provided by registered lobbyists to ensure accuracy; reviewing allegations of non-registration or misconduct by lobbyists, and carrying out formal investigations. Although this expenditure is similar to the budget for education and research, it must be remembered that it does not include any criminal investigations and prosecutions which may follow from the work carried out in the Office. Another approach to comparing the relative costs and benefits of education *versus* investigation, is to compare the number of individuals who can be reached through education with the number who would either immediately affected or aware of the consequences of investigations. Enforcement investigations can be time consuming and labour intensive, relatively few can be completed each year. On the other hand strategically targeted information sessions for senior officials, coupled with increased exposure to lobbying regulation during in-service education programmes, reaches a much larger group of public servants. Add special programmes for lobbyists and for the general public, and the level of exposure and awareness grows considerably. In the words Michael Nelson, Canada's Registrar of Lobbyists, "while enforcement spending is necessary and may be effective in creating individual remedies, it does not provide the reach and leverage that education spending does, and is thus not as efficient as a way to spend the regulatory dollar" (e-mail. M. Nelson to P. Pross, 20 March 2007).

56. For example, the recent changes to Canada's lobbying rules introduced by the Federal Accountability Act which require lobbyists to provide monthly reports on certain communications with designated public office holders has caused consternation in Ottawa lobbying circles. During the summer of 2006 *The Lobby Monitor* reported that lobbyists were campaigning "on the golf courses of the nation's capital" with "talking points focused on the costs of compliance, the administrative nightmare that would ensue and the erosion of client... privacy" ("Lobby Notes", 25 September 2006, p. 2). Those who hire Ottawa lobbyists should hope that they are more successful on their clients' behalf, than were on their own. In Washington, firms that have specialised in taking advantage of the practice of "earmarking" will doubtless find that recent changes to regulations which have the effect of limiting the use of this practice will force them to adopt other strategies. K-Street lobbyists are infinitely nimble and doubtless will overcome this difficulty.

57. In Canada, for example, *The Hill Times* and *The Lobby Monitor* provide this service.

58. In recent years these concerns have been extended to the families of public officials. Currently in the United States, for example, there is debate over how to regulate lobbying by the spouses of legislators.

59. For an account of the Abramoff affair, and one view of an appropriate reform agenda, see Continetti, *The K Street Gang*.

Bibliography

Assemblée Nationale (2008), 13th Legislature, *Proposition de Résolution n° 156, Assemblée Nationale, Communiqué de Presse*, France.

Assemblée Nationale (2009), New Article 26, Paragraph III-B, *L'Instruction générale du Bureau*, adopted by the Bureau on 2 July 2009, France, *www.assemblee-nationale.fr/representants-interets/index.asp#article26.*

Canadian Government (1995), "An Act to Amend the Lobbyists Registration Act", Statutes of Canada, Chapter 12, Section 4.2.c.

Chenier, John (ed.) (2003), *The Lobby Monitor*, 15 (29 October 2003) 1, pp. 6-7.

Clarke, S. (1991), "Regulation of Lobbying in Foreign Countries", Washington DC: Law Library of Congress, mimeo.

Commission of the European Union Communities (2007), "Follow-up to the Green Paper 'European Transparency Initiative'", Com. (2007) 127, Communication from the Commission.

Congressional Research Service (1986), Library of Congress, "Congress and Pressure Groups: Lobbying in a Modern Democracy: A Report Prepared for the Subcommittee on Intergovernmental Relations of the Committee on Governmental Affairs", United States Senate, Washington DC: US Government Printing Office, pp. 5, 43, 44.

Continetti, M. (2006), *The K Street Gang*, NY: Doubleday, p. 243.

Crespo Allen, Marilia (1996), "Rules on Lobbying and Intergroups in the National Parliaments of the Member States", W5/rev., National Parliaments Series, Working Document, European Parliament, Directorate General for Research, Brussels.

European Commission (2006), "Green Paper of the European Transparency Initiative", COM(2006) 194 final, *http://ec.europa.eu/transparency/eti/docs/gp_en.pdf.*

European Commission (2008), *Draft: A Code of Conduct for Interest Representatives, http//ec.europa.eu/transparency/consultation_code/docs/gp_en.pdf.*

European Parliament (2007), "Draft Report on the Development of the Framework for the Activities of Interest Representatives (Lobbyists) in the European Institutions", 2007/2115(INI), Draft Report.

Government of British Columbia (2003), "A Guide to the Lobbyists Registration Act", Office of the Registrar, p. 7.

Government of Tuscany, Italy (2002), Regional Law No. 5 of 18 January 2002, Rules for ensuring the political and administrative transparency of the Regional Council of Tuscany.

Greenwood, J. (2004), "Regulation of Interest Representation in the European Union (EU)", *Research Guide to US and International Interest Groups*, Praeger Publishers, Westport Connecticut, p. 379.

Herrmann, Frederick M. (2006), "Lobbying in New Jersey, 2006", paper presented at the Nineteenth Annual Meeting of the Northeastern Regional Conference on Lobbying in Philadelphia, Pennsylvania, New Jersey Election Law Enforcement Commission, August 2006.

Hrebenar *et al.* (1998), "Lobby Regulation in the Japanese Diet", *Parliamentary Affairs*, Vol. 51, No. 4, Oxford University Press, Oxford, pp. 551-558, 555-7, 556-7.

Hurse, Carl (2008), "House Creates a Panel to Watch over Lawmakers' Behaviour", *New York Times*, 12 March 2008.

Johnston, David (2006), "FBI's Focus on Public Corruption Includes 2 000 Investigations", *New York Times*, 11 May 2006.

Jordan, Grant (1998), "Towards Regulation in the UK: From 'General Good Sense' to 'Formalised Rules'", *Parliamentary Affairs*, 51 (1998) 4, Oxford University Press, Oxford, pp. 524-37, 526.

Kirkpatrick, David (2006), "When Lobbyists Say 'I Do', Should They Add 'I Won't?'", *New York Times*, 19 February 2006.

Loree G., Bykerk (2004), "Consumer Groups", *Research Guide to US and International Interest Groups*, Praeger Publishers, Westport Connecticut.

Malone, M. (2004), "Regulation of Lobbyists in Developed Countries: Current Rules and Practices", Report, Institute of Public Administration, Dublin, Ireland, pp. 3, 12.

O'Donnell, John (2007), "The RPSEA Rip-Off: How the Natural Gas Industry Extracted a Billion-Dollar Boondoggle from Congress", Report, Washington DC: Public Citizen, Washington DC.

OECD (2006), "Lobbying: Key Policy Issues", internal working document, Public Governance and Territorial Development Directorate, OECD, Paris.

Parliament of Canada (1987), House of Commons, Standing Committee on Elections, Privileges and Procedure, Issue No. 2, First Report, "Respecting (in respect of?) Lobbying and the Registration of Paid Lobbyists", 25 January, pp. 2-3 and 2-6.

Pross, A.P. (1991), "The Rise of the Lobbying Issue in Canada", *Commercial Lobbyists: Politics for Profit in Britain*, Aberdeen, University of Aberdeen Press.

Rechtman, R. and J. Panum Larsen-Ledet (1998), "Regulation of Lobbyists in Scandinavia: A Danish Perspective", *Parliamentary Affairs*, 51, 4, pp. 579-86.

Ronit, K. and V. Schneider (1998), "The Strange Case of Regulating Lobbying in Germany", *Parliamentary Affairs*, 51, 4, Oxford University Press, Oxford, pp. 559-78.

Samuels, D. (2006), "What, No Tipping the People's Servants?", *New York Times*, 27 November.

The Lobby Monitor (2006), 18 December, pp. 1-2.

Thomas, C. (ed.) (2004), *Research Guide to US and International Interest Groups*, Praeger Publishers, Westport Connecticut, pp. 379-381, 379-385, 374-377.

Toronto Globe and Mail (1999), "Giving money to politicians necessary: Fermco", 18 December, p. A4.

US General Accounting Office (1990), "Foreign Agent Registration: Justice Needs to Improve Program Administration", GAO/NSIAD-90-250, Washington DC, GAO Report to the Chairman, Subcommittee on Oversight of Government, Committee on Governmental Affairs, US Senate.

US House of Representatives (1995), Committee on the Judiciary (Mr. Canaday) Report: The Lobbying Disclosure Act of 1995 104th Congress, 1st Session, Report 104-339, p. 13.

Warhurst, John (1998), "Locating the Target: Regulating Lobbying in Australia", *Parliamentary Affairs*, 51 (1998) 4, Oxford University Press, Oxford, 538-50.

Weisman, J. and J.H. Birnbaum (2007), "Senate Passes Ethics Package", *Washington Post*, 19 January 2007.

Chapter 3

Canada's Federal Lobbying Legislation: Evolution and Operation of the Lobbyists Registration Act[1]

This chapter outlines the purpose and key elements of the legislation on lobbying at the federal level in Canada. It describes the stages in the evolution of provisions for enhancing transparency of lobbying through requiring registration and reporting.

The chapter also provides information on organisational and procedural frameworks, as well as the measures taken to put the Lobbyists Registration Act and the Lobbyists' Code of Conduct into effect and enforce compliance.

Finally, the chapter summarises major features of the new strengthened legislation and the powers of the Commissioner of Lobbying in charge of the implementation of the new Lobbying Act, which came into force on 2 July 2008.

Summary

Canada has more than a decade of experience in implementing legislation on lobbying. Over time, growing expectations of transparency and integrity have brought lobbying back repeatedly to the political agenda. The Lobbyists Registration Act (the Act, or LRA), Canada's federal legislation regarding the registration of lobbyists, came into force in 1989. This chapter summarises the operation of the Act, as described in the Registrar of Lobbyists' annual reports to Parliament and other public documents such as the *Main Estimates*. Although the emphasis is on recent experience, important changes made by the legislator are pointed out where appropriate to show how the Act has evolved. The most recent amendments to the Act brought by the FAA[2] are described here in order to provide a complete picture of the evolution of Canadian federal lobbying legislation.

Purpose and description of the Lobbyists Registration Act

The Lobbyists Registration Act provides for the public registration of those individuals who are paid to communicate with public office holders with regard to certain matters as described in the legislation (*i.e.* lobbying). Public office holders are defined in the Act as virtually all persons occupying an elected or appointed position in the Government of Canada, including members of the House of Commons and the Senate and their staff, as well as officers and employees of federal departments and agencies, members of the Canadian Forces and members of the Royal Canadian Mounted Police (RCMP).

Basic principles

Four basic principles are set out in the preamble to the Act:

- Free and open access to government is an important matter of public interest.
- Lobbying public office holders is a legitimate activity.
- It is desirable that public office holders and the general public be able to know who is engaged in lobbying activities.
- The system for the registration of paid lobbyists should not impede free and open access to government.

Individuals are required to **register under the Act** if they communicate with federal public office holders, whether formally or informally, with regard to:

- the making, developing or amending of federal legislative proposals, bills or resolutions, regulations, policies or programmes;
- the awarding of federal grants, contributions or other financial benefits; and
- in the case of consultant lobbyists, the awarding of a federal government contract or arranging a meeting between their client and a public office holder.

Three categories of lobbyists

The Act provides for three categories of lobbyists:

- consultant lobbyists;
- in-house lobbyists (corporations); and
- in-house lobbyists (organisations).

Consultant lobbyists are individuals who, for payment, lobby on behalf of a client. Consultant lobbyists may be government-relations consultants, lawyers, accountants or other professional advisors who provide lobbying services for their clients. They must file a registration for each individual undertaking (*i.e.* for each lobbying contract). When they complete the undertaking, they must advise the Registrar. The registration information remains on the registry; however, it is then displayed as "inactive".

In-house lobbyists (corporations) are employees of corporations that carry out commercial activities for financial gain; they lobby as a significant part of their duties. These employees are usually full-time officers who devote a significant part of their duties to public affairs or government-relations work. The most senior paid officer must register the corporation if the total lobbying activity of all employees equals 20% or more of the duties of one equivalent full-time employee. The registration must include the names of all senior officers – the most senior officer and all his or her direct subordinates – who engage in any lobbying activity, as well as the name of any employee who devotes a significant part of his or her duties to lobbying activities.

In-house lobbyists (organisations) are employees of not-for-profit organisations, such as associations and universities. The most senior paid officer of such an organisation must register the names of all employees engaged in lobbying activity if the total lobbying activity of all such employees equals 20% or more of the duties of one equivalent full-time employee.

All lobbyists are required to **disclose certain information** within time limits specified in the Act. This information includes:

- the names of their clients, or corporate or organisational employers;
- the names of the parent or subsidiary companies that would benefit from the lobbying activity;

- the organisational members of coalition groups;
- the specific subject matters lobbied;
- the names of the federal departments or agencies contacted;
- the sources and amounts of any government funding received; and
- the communication techniques used, such as meetings, telephone calls, electronic communications, or grassroots lobbying.

Corporations and organisations must also provide general descriptions of their business or activities.

The Lobbyists' Code of Conduct

When the Act was amended by Parliament in 1995, provision was made for a code of conduct for lobbyists. The Lobbyists' Code of Conduct[3] (the Code) came into force on 1 March 1997.

The purpose of the Lobbyists' Code of Conduct is to assure the Canadian public that lobbying is carried out ethically and according to the highest standards. This is in order to conserve and **enhance public confidence and trust** in the integrity, objectivity and impartiality of government decision making.

The Code establishes mandatory standards of conduct for all lobbyists communicating with Government of Canada public office holders. The Lobbyists' Code of Conduct begins with a preamble that states its purpose and places it in a broader context.

Principles and rules

Next, a body of overriding Principles sets out, in positive terms, the goals and objectives to be attained, without establishing precise standards. These **Principles of Integrity, Honesty, Openness and Professionalism** represent goals that should be pursued, and are intended as general guidance.

The Code's Principles are followed by Rules that set out specific obligations and requirements. The rules are organised into three categories:

- transparency;
- confidentiality; and
- conflict of Interest.

Under the Rule of Transparency, lobbyists have an obligation to provide accurate information to public office holders; they must also disclose the identity of the persons or organisations on whose behalf the representation is made, as well as the purpose of the representation. They must also disclose to their clients, employers or organisations their obligations under the Lobbyists Registration Act and the Code itself. Under the Rule of Confidentiality, lobbyists must neither divulge confidential information nor use insider information to the disadvantage of their clients, employers or organisations. Finally, under the Rule of Conflict of

Interest, lobbyists must not use improper influence nor represent conflicting or competing interests without the consent of their clients.

The Lobbyists' Code of Conduct is an integral part of the disclosure and ethical requirements that apply to all lobbyists.

Lobbyists, their registration and disclosures

The Registry of Lobbyists is the Act's core instrument of transparency. Registry information collected under the Act and the Lobbyists Registration Regulations is a matter of public record so that information about who is being paid to communicate with federal public office holders is available. Accessible over the Internet,[4] the Registry is well-known and heavily used by lobbyists, journalists, public office holders, citizens and others. **The Registry has evolved since 1989** in terms of the disclosures it contains, as well as the means of making that data available.

The 1989 version of the Act distinguished between only two types of lobbyists, rather than the three described earlier in this chapter. **Tier I lobbyists** were essentially the same group now known as consultant lobbyists. They were required to disclose relatively few details compared to current requirements. Disclosures were limited to their clients and the subject matter of the undertaking, as well as the parents and subsidiaries if the client was a corporation.

Tier II lobbyists were employees who were paid to lobby on behalf of their employer. These lobbyists were required to disclose even less information that those in Tier I. Only the name and address of the employer was required.

Amendments made in 1995 to registration requirements

In 1995, the Lobbyists Registration Act was amended. The amended Act strengthened the disclosure requirements to make more meaningful and comprehensive information about lobbyists, and what they do, available to all. The new registration requirements came into force on 31 January 1996.

The changes to the Act provided for the three categories of lobbyists that exist to this day. The former Tier I or professional lobbyists were now known as consultant lobbyists. The former Tier II or employee lobbyists were subdivided into in-house lobbyists (corporations) and in-house lobbyists (organisations). The former group included for-profit entities; and the latter, not-for-profit entities such as universities, professional associations and interest groups.

For organisations, the senior officer must register as an in-house lobbyist (organisations):

- when one or more employees communicate with federal public office holders in an attempt to influence government decisions; and

- where the accumulated activity of all such employees would constitute a significant part of the duties of one employee.

Registration is required for the same activities as for consultant lobbyists, except for lobbying in respect of the awarding of a contract.

More disclosure

All lobbyists were required to disclose certain information within time limits specified by the law. The information required under the amended legislation was much more extensive than that required prior to 31 January 1996, and included:

- the name or description of the specific legislative proposals, bills, regulations, policies, programmes, grants, contributions or contracts sought;
- the names of the federal departments or other governmental institutions lobbied;
- the source and amount of any government funding; and
- the communication techniques used, such as grassroots lobbying.

Corporations and organisations also had to provide a general description of their business or activities.

Revision in 2005 to strengthen and simplify registration

In 2005, further legislative changes that affected the disclosures in the Registry came into force. The revised Act broadened the scope of activities for which registration is required by removing the expression "in an attempt to influence" from the Act as it had previously read. This meant that **all communications** covered by the legislation now constituted lobbying and, therefore, required registration.

The new legislation strengthened and simplified the registration requirements set out in the Act. It did so by:

- requiring all lobbyists to update or renew their filings every six months; and
- implementing a single filing approach for the registration of corporations and not-for-profit organisations.

Previously, accountability for registration of in-house (corporations) lobbyists rested with the individual lobbyist. The amendments **shifted this accountability to the most senior officer** in the corporation. This single filing system was intended to provide consistent treatment for all types of lobbyists, as established under the Act, and to ensure that responsibility for the actions of lobbyists rested at the highest corporate levels.

The amended Act also required former public office holders engaged in lobbying to provide information on the positions they held within the federal government. Finally, the revised Act clarified minor discrepancies that previously existed between the French and English versions of the legislation.

The Registry of Lobbyists

The original Registry of Lobbyists introduced in 1989 was a paper-based system. However, as the Government of Canada made progress throughout the 1990s with its initiatives to make government information and services available online, it became clear that the Registry of Lobbyists would be an excellent candidate.

Electronic filing

Amendments made to the Act in 1995 permitted lobbyists to file their returns electronically, via the Office of the Registrar's dial-up filing system. The electronic filing system was designed to enable contact from the most basic computer equipment and to **support virtually all makes of computers**. Lobbyists needed only a computer, modem and communications software to access the bilingual application. To ensure that only authorised users were given access to the system, a contractual agreement was developed which identified the lobbyist's responsibility for **electronic certification** using a system of passwords. Organisations or companies that did not yet have the necessary equipment could file electronically using the facilities within the Office of the Registrar of Lobbyists (ORL).

To encourage lobbyists to file their registration forms electronically, the Office offered use of this technology free of charge and introduced a fee schedule to process filings made in paper format.

Currently, more than **99% of the transactions performed** in the Registry of Lobbyists (registrations, amendments, renewals, and terminations) are carried out **electronically** through the Lobbyists Registration System (LRS). The LRS is a now web-based application available to lobbyists and the public through the Internet. It is used both for processing and disclosing registrations filed by lobbyists.

Registration information

The interactive system validates basic data, such as names and addresses; reminds lobbyists to complete all required information; and permits lobbyists to easily edit their own disclosures. Data, once verified, are moved to the Registry database. **Anyone may search this database** for information and produce reports from their own computer.

Users can search and retrieve information on:

- who lobbies for which firms, corporations, organisations or associations;
- the parent and subsidiary companies or corporations that may benefit from the lobbying;
- the organisational members of coalition groups;
- the activities that corporations and associations engage in (a general description);
- the government of Canada departments or agencies being contacted;
- the names or descriptions of the specific legislative proposals, bills, regulations, policies, programmes, grants, contributions or contracts being sought; and
- the positions former public office holders have held with the government of Canada.

Users can also produce their own summary reports on registered lobbyists, as well as copies of individual registration forms, directly from the Registry. It is also possible to access a list of recent registrations that includes all new registrations, amendments and terminations processed within the previous 30 days. Users who search and retrieve the data directly from their own computers may do so free of charge.

Registration statistics

Registration statistics are reported to Parliament each year by the Registrar. These statistics include, volume and type of lobbyist registrations, subject matter of lobbying activities, and government institutions lobbied.

From the start of its operation in 1989, the Registry of Lobbyists contained a high volume of transactions. Within ten days of the launch of the Registry, 829 Tier I registration forms had been received. Within two months, 1 709 Tier II registrations had been filed. By the end of the first fiscal year of operation, 6 221 registrations had been processed for a total of 2 828 lobbyists.

An exceptional increase of registrations in 2005-06

Registration volumes fluctuated over the next several years but, the changes were not dramatic, with one exception during the 2005-06 reporting period. That year, a combination of factors contributed to a **sharp rise** – 847% – in the number of registered in-house corporate lobbyists. A detailed analysis of this rise has not been carried out. However, **contributing factors** may have included the prominence of lobbying-related stories in the media; the implementation of new, stronger lobbying legislation in 2005; an increase in resources provided to the Registrar; and a general increase in awareness of registration requirements.

Table 3.1 and Table 3.2 show the volume of lobbyists and registrations in March 2008.

Table 3.1. **Active lobbyists lobbying the Canadian government**

Consultant lobbyists	874
In-house corporation lobbyists	1 729
In-house organisation lobbyists	2 432
Total lobbyists	**5 035**

Table 3.2. **Active registrations in Canada as at 25 March 2008**

Consultant registrations	2 878
In-house corporation registrations	282
In-house organisation registrations	439
Total active registrations	**3 599**

The Act requires that lobbyists of all three types disclose the areas of concern (subject matters) of their lobbying activity. Table 3.3 gives statistics of the top 20 areas of concern in March 2008.

Table 3.3. **Areas of concern in active registrations in Canada**

Area of concern	Active registrations
Industry	1 813
Taxation and finance	1 381
Environment	1 184
International trade	1 147
Health	1 041
Science and technology	949
Transportation	782
Consumer issues	779
Employment and training	740
Energy	737
Regional development	714
Government procurement	658
Infrastructure	582
International relations	559
Agriculture	546
Aboriginal affairs	530
Defence	523
Intellectual property	493
Internal trade	477
Financial institutions	457

The Lobbyists Registration Act requires that lobbyists of all three types disclose the names of government institutions that are the subject of their lobbying activity. Table 3.4 shows the statistics in March 2008 on the top 20 institutions lobbied.

Table 3.4. **Canadian government organisations in active registrations**

Department or agency	Active registrations
Industry Canada (IC)	2 210
Finance Canada (FIN)	1 663
Members of the House of Commons	1 426
Privy Council Office (PCO)	1 375
Foreign Affairs and International Trade (DFAIT)	1 220
Environment Canada (EC)	1 206
Health Canada (HC)	1 118
Prime Minister's Office (PMO)	1 044
Transport Canada (TC)	898
Treasury Board of Canada (TBS)	855
Natural Resources Canada (NRCan)	814
Revenue Canada (RC)	775
Public Works and Government Services Canada (PWGSC)	746
Agriculture and Agri-Food Canada (AAFC)	690
Human Resources Development Canada (HRDC)	664
Indian and Northern Affairs Canada (INAC)	648
National Defence (DND)	638
Canadian Heritage (PCH)	602
Senate of Canada	544
Justice Canada (JC)	504

Enforcement

The Act provides for various types of **penalties and sanctions**. Contraventions of the Act or its regulations are subject on summary conviction to a fine of up to CAD 25 000. Individuals who knowingly make false or misleading statements in any return or other document submitted to the Registrar are subject on summary conviction to a fine of up to CAD 25 000, imprisonment for up to six months, or both. Individuals who knowingly make false or misleading statements in any return or other document submitted to the Registrar are subject on indictment to a fine of up to CAD 100 000, imprisonment for up to two years, or both. Proceedings by way of summary conviction related to these offences must be instituted not later than two years after the offence.

The first significant test of the penalties under the Act came in 1999 and revealed an important weakness in the Act. Allegations of unregistered lobbying were brought to the attention of the Registrar and the Ethics Counsellor. These allegations were then forwarded to the RCMP for further investigation. The RCMP determined that they did not believe that they would be able to secure a conviction because it **would be too difficult to prove** to the court that the alleged lobbyist had acted, "with the intent to influence" a public office holder. Consequently, the Act could not be effectively enforced. This development led to an important amendment to the Act in 2005 that removed the phrase "with the intent to influence" from the legislation.

The current ORL enforces the Act in a number of ways: the registration process, media monitoring, advisory letters, administrative reviews, investigations and strategic enforcement.

Registration process

The registration process is an important point of enforcement. The Office **provides assistance** in relation to the registration process, reminds lobbyists to renew their registrations, and **verifies** that disclosures are consistent and complete. Information provided by lobbyists, such as clients, parent companies or subsidiaries of companies, is analysed by office staff and verified where necessary. Questions on the content of disclosures are sent by email to registrants and the registration is not approved until the Office is satisfied with the accuracy and transparency of the disclosure. This requires an efficient process and diligent staff because volumes are very high. For example, during fiscal year 2006-07, 9 656 registrations were processed, of which 7 775 were consultant lobbyist registrations, 793 were in-house lobbyist (corporations) registrations and 1 088 were in-house lobbyist (organisations) registrations.

Media monitoring

Media monitoring is carried out on a regular basis. The Office uses a sophisticated web-based monitoring system to **examine the content of articles** in media publications that mention lobbying activities. Follow-up is done by staff in the Investigations Directorate to determine if alleged lobbying is the subject of a valid registration.

Advisory letters

Advisory letters are sent to individuals or organisations for which media monitoring or other information received by the Office indicates that unregistered lobbying may be taking place. These letters advise the recipients that they may have obligations under the Act. This practice is designed to **enhance the awareness** of organisations and corporations regarding the Act and to encourage them to visit the ORL website[5] or contact the ORL directly for additional information pertaining to registration requirements.

Administrative reviews

Administrative reviews are initiated following requests or complaints received from external sources alleging a possible contravention of the Act or the Code. Administrative reviews are also initiated as a result of in-house monitoring by the ORL. An administrative review is not a formal investigation. Its purpose is to **assemble and check factual evidence**, with a view to determining if a formal investigation is required. All information gathered during either an administrative review or an investigation is retained in accordance with government information management practices.

An administrative review typically involves:

- reviewing all registration files in the custody of the ORL, available correspondence and other forms of communication between the ORL and the lobbyist; and
- confirming, by phone or in-person interviews with public office holders, whether registration activities have indeed taken place. The ORL may also decide to contact the lobbyist during the course of a review.

Some examples of allegations that have resulted in the initiation of an administrative review are:

- allegations of unregistered lobbying activities and breaches of the Code by a number of lobbyists, acting on behalf of an organisation, who were communicating with a government department to seek federal funding. The individuals in question are alleged to have breached all three principles of the Lobbyists' Code of Conduct – namely Integrity and Honesty, Openness, and Professionalism – and, additionally, are alleged to have not provided accurate information in registering;
- an allegation of improper disclosure of government funding by several organisations;
- allegations that employees of a public broadcasting advocacy group were engaged in unregistered lobbying activities;
- an allegation that a voluntary, charitable organisation, which promotes personal health across Canada and in developing countries, failed to register receipt of financial benefits from a government institution; and
- an allegation that a lobbyist's registration did not contain information that he would be lobbying members of Parliament.

At the end of March 2008, 34 administrative reviews were underway.

If a review indicates there are reasonable grounds to believe a breach of the Act has occurred within the two-year limitation period of the Act, the Registrar of Lobbyists is informed of the conclusions and the matter is referred to the Royal Canadian Mounted Police (RCMP). Alleged breaches of the Code by registered lobbyists are dealt with by the Registrar, who will determine if an investigation pursuant to the Code of Conduct is required.

Investigations

Investigations of alleged breaches of the Lobbyists' Code of Conduct are **carried out by the Registrar, who has significant investigative powers**, identical to those of a superior court of record. These powers include the ability to summon and enforce the attendance of persons so that they may give evidence under oath, and to compel them to produce documents. Once the Registrar has completed such an investigation, he or she must submit a copy to the Registrar General of Canada, who must cause it to be tabled in each House of Parliament. At the end of March 2008, ten investigations had been initiated, and four completed. The four were successfully challenged in the federal court by the individual who was the subject of the investigations. The Registrar has launched an appeal of this decision.

Strategic Enforcement

Strategic Enforcement is the term used by the Registrar to describe the Office's efforts to extend its reach. The Registrar believes that by making the requirements of the Act and the Code of Conduct better known not only lobbyists, but to public office holders and those who employ lobbyists, great leverage in enforcement of the legislation can be obtained. From an efficiency and effectiveness perspective, **a dollar spent on education and awareness has more potential to contribute to enforcement than a dollar spent pursuing an investigation**. As a practical example, if a public office holder is made aware of the registration requirements of the Act and is encouraged to ask a potential lobbyist if he or she is registered, a possible infraction and the expensive costs of pursuing an investigation may be averted.

Education and awareness

The ORL believes that education and awareness are essential to compliance with the LRA.

From the earliest days of the LRA's existence, successive Registrars have made public speaking appearances and the distribution of educational materials a part of their communication activities. More recently, with more staff and resources available, the Office has used several means to promote awareness of the Act and its requirements, including:

- direct communication;
- the ORL website;
- training and information sessions;

- media relations;
- conferences and learning events;
- presentations to departmental management teams and staff; and
- dialogue with other jurisdictions.

Direct communications

The ORL **responds to inquiries** from lobbyists, the media and the public on a daily basis. Updates about the Registry are provided to registered lobbyists via email and through notices to registrants on the Office's website.

In order to improve communications with registrants, the Operations Directorate organises **outreach and information sessions** with lobbying firms, with a view to improving the overall quality and reliability of disclosures filed in the Registry of Lobbyists.

The ORL website

ORL staff devotes considerable effort to improving the ORL's website,[6] giving it a clearer, fresher appearance, and making it a more useful information and communications tool. An updated version of the site, which is easier to navigate, was launched in 2006-07. New sections were created for information documents, such as **reports, presentations, interpretation bulletins and advisory opinions**, which are updated or added on a regular basis. The ORL recorded 74 792 visits to its website in 2006-07, with 379 720 pages accessed.

Training and information sessions

While the ORL does not have the resources to deliver extensive training programmes, it presents information sessions to interested groups and organisations outside the federal government. For example, the Registrar has participated in an information session on a proposed (and currently operating) lobbyist's registry for the City of Toronto. Senior Office staff presented information sessions to groups of lobbyists and to organisations that expressed interest in becoming registered under the Act. Senior Office staff also provided briefing sessions about the Canadian federal regime to foreign delegations, for example, from the Norwegian Parliament and the Korean Independent Commission Against Corruption.

Media relations

On a regular basis, the ORL responds to inquiries from the media about the Registry. The Office provides clarification about the registration process, investigations, and administrative reviews to the extent permissible under the Act and under privacy provisions.

Conferences and learning events

Each year, the Registrar and senior ORL staff take part in conferences and panel discussions in the National Capital Region and elsewhere in Canada. In past years these have included the Access and Privacy Conference, hosted by the University of Alberta in Edmonton, the Annual University Government Relations Officers' Meeting in Winnipeg, the Public Affairs Association of Canada Conference and the Canadian Council for Public-Private Partnerships National Conference, both of which were held in Toronto.

Briefings for federal government institutions

The ORL provides outreach within the federal government through briefings to management at departments and other federal organisations. These sessions, provided at the organisations' request, are aimed at:

- assisting public office holders in becoming familiar with the provisions of the Act and the Code; and
- addressing issues faced by specific organisations regarding lobbying and interactions with lobbyists.

Dialogue with other jurisdictions

The ORL exchanges ideas and practices with counterparts from other Canadian and international jurisdictions. Meetings have been held with officials from Quebec, Nova Scotia, Ontario and British Columbia, with US counterparts and with officials from the Organisation for Economic Co-operation and Development (OECD) and its member countries.

Organisation, resources and priorities

Organisation

The structure of what is now the ORL has **evolved considerably** since its inception. For the first years of its existence, the Office was situated within the Department of Consumer and Corporate Affairs. Machinery changes within the government eventually led to the Office residing within the Department of Industry in an organisation called the Office of the Ethics Counsellor.

In 1995, amendments to the Act provided the Ethics Counsellor with responsibility for, among other duties, enforcement of the new Lobbyists Code of Conduct. The Registrar of Lobbyists retained responsibility for the Registry. Over time, the structural arrangement of the Ethics Counsellor having Lobbyists' Code of Conduct responsibilities in addition to other duties, as well as the reporting relationship to the Prime Minister, were subject to criticism. In 2004, the Act was amended, setting in motion the most substantial changes in structure and resources in the Act's history.

The 2004 amendments to the Act gave the Registrar for the first time, responsibility for both operation of the Registry and for the Lobbyists' Code of Conduct. An Assistant Deputy Minister within Industry Canada was designated as Registrar of Lobbyists – the first time that the position had been held by such a senior public servant. A new ORL was established within Industry Canada.

Further significant changes followed soon after. In September 2005, the Registrar of Lobbyists was made into a **full-time position**. This measure was taken in response to the increased workload resulting from the coming into force in the summer of 2005 of amendments to the Act. Immediately after the full-time appointment, the Registrar took a number of steps to transform what was known as the Lobbyists Registration Branch of Industry Canada into a more independent organisation. The Registrar ceased all participation in Industry Canada's management team and, in October 2005, moved the Branch, now renamed the ORL, to new premises physically separated from those of Industry Canada.

In an effort to increase the efficiency of the registration process and to strengthen the enforcement capabilities of the Office, the Registrar undertook a restructuring of the organisation by creating two directorates focused on groups of core activities. An **Investigation Directorate** was established, the major role of which was to enforce the Act through conducting administrative reviews, investigations, and policy analysis related to the application of the Act. The Registrar also decided to combine a number of responsibilities within an Operations Directorate. This new unit now performed all registration functions, including client service, advice, interpretation and informatics, as well as communications and certain corporate functions.

In February 2006, the Prime Minister announced that the ORL had been transferred from the Industry portfolio to the Treasury Board portfolio as a stand-alone office, to increase its independence while the Government was working to further revise and strengthen the LRA. Since that time, the ORL has been a **separate and independent department** and the Registrar of Lobbyists has had the authority of a deputy head.

Resources and priorities

The expansion of the ORL described above was made possible by a **substantial budget increase approved by Parliament**.

Initial resources allocated to the ORL in 1989 had included a budget of CAD 467 000 and a staff of four. Budgets varied little over the years although the budget allocated to the new Registrar in 2004 had dwindled to CAD 313 000 to cover all operational expenses and salaries.

The budget approved by Parliament for 2006-07 was CAD 3.5 million annually and a staff of 20 to operate the ORL. The approval was based on three priorities to be pursued by the Office. They were to:

- **Update the Registry and enhance its transparency** – When the on-line Registry was launched in 1996, it was not designed for the volumes of data it now contains, nor for the search expectations of current Internet users. Improving the capacity of the Registry and preparing it for enhanced capabilities was a priority for the planning period.
- **Increase awareness** of Lobbyists Registration Act and Lobbyists' Code of Conduct requirements – As mentioned earlier in this chapter, the Registrar believed that increasing awareness of the Lobbyists Registration Act, including how it operates and who needs to register, was key to increasing compliance. Parliament was asked for resources to begin developing a comprehensive education and awareness strategy aimed at public office holders, lobbyists and those who employ them.
- **Pursue enforcement and communicate the results** – The Registrar had commenced several investigations under the Lobbyists' Code of Conduct. It was seen as important not only to pursue enforcement by assigning more resources to reviews and investigations within the Office, but also to communicate the outcomes of enforcement activity.

The broad strategic outcome of these priorities was to contribute to confidence in the integrity of government decision making through transparency and accountability in the lobbying of public office holders.

The Lobbying Act

Bill C-2, the FAA, received Royal Assent on 12 December 2006, as S.C. 2006 Chapter 9, setting the stage for amendments to the Lobbyists Registration Act. The Lobbyists Registration Act was renamed the Lobbying Act[7] and includes **important changes**. Among these are:

- the appointment of an **independent Commissioner of Lobbying** with a strong mandate to investigate violations of the Lobbying Act and the Lobbyists' Code of Conduct;
- a **five-year ban** on lobbying for ministers, ministerial staff, and senior public servants once they leave office, as well as for members of Prime Ministers' transition teams;
- a ban on the payment and receipt of success or **contingency fees**;
- requirements that **communications** with certain designated public office holders be recorded; and

- **expanded investigative powers** for the Commissioner of Lobbying and a longer period under which lobbying violations may be investigated and prosecuted.

The ORL supported the work of Parliament as it considered Bill C-2 by appearing before the committees of the House of Commons and the Senate to provide testimony on the operational implications of the Bill. Subsequent to Royal Assent, the Office began preparing for implementation of the lobbying provisions. Chief among these are enhancements to the LRS. The Lobbying Act came into force on 2 July 2008.

Notes

1. This chapter was prepared by Michael Nelson, Registrar of Lobbyists, Canada.
2. The Federal Accountability Act received Royal Assent on 12 December 2006 (*www.faa-lfi.gc.ca/index_e.asp*). It strengthens legislation under the new Lobbying Act. The full text of the Federal Accountability Act can be seen at *www2.parl.gc.ca/HousePublications/Publication.aspx?Parl=39&Ses=1&Mode=1&Pub=Bill&Doc=C-2_4&Language=E*.
3. The full text of the Lobbyists' Code of Conduct can be consulted at *www.ocl-cal.gc.ca/epic/site/lobbyist-lobbyiste1.nsf/en/nx00019e.html*.
4. The Public Registry of Lobbyists is available at *www.ocl-cal.gc.ca/epic/site/lobbyist-lobbyiste1.nsf/en/h_nx00274e.html*.
5. As of 2 July 2008, the Commissioner of Lobbying site is available at *www.ocl-cal.gc.ca/epic/site/lobbyist-lobbyiste1.nsf/Intro*.
6. The portal of the Office of the Registrar of Lobbyists (as of 2 July 2008, the Commissioner of Lobbying) is available at *www.ocl-cal.gc.ca/epic/site/lobbyist-lobbyiste1.nsf/Intro*.
7. A consolidated version of the new Lobbying Act can be consulted at *www.ocl-cal.gc.ca/epic/site/lobbyist-lobbyiste1.nsf/en/h_nx00270e.html*.

Lobbyists, Governments and Public Trust, Volume 1
Increasing Transparency through Legislation

Chapter 4

Quebec's Experience: Developing a Legal Framework for Lobbying and Lobbyist Registration[1]

This chapter outlines the regulation and monitoring of lobbying activities at the sub-national level. It reviews the solutions in place in Quebec for designing and implementing the Lobbying Transparency and Ethics Act. Sections address the following key questions:

- *Why regulate lobbying?*
- *What activities should be considered lobbying and what should be covered by the regulation?*
- *What obligations are to be imposed, and on whom, in the context of a lobbying relationship?*
- *What type of control mechanisms are necessary to ensure compliance?*

Summary

This chapter[2] outlines Quebec's recent experience in regulating and monitoring lobbying. It describes the **main implications of developing and implementing a legal framework** for enhancing transparency and accountability in lobbying at the sub-national level. The chapter addresses four basic questions inherent to any legislative attempt at regulating lobbying:

- Why regulate lobbying?
- What is to be considered lobbying for the purpose of such regulation?
- What obligations are to be imposed, and on whom, in the context of a lobbying relationship?
- What type of control mechanisms are to be set up in order to ensure compliance?

Why regulate lobbying?

Lobbying is often depicted in a negative way, as a sort of obscure undue influence by private or vested interests in the decision-making processes of public institutions. If this picture were true, then the logical step would be to consider prohibiting lobbying altogether. Needless to say, that it is a gross misconception of the reality of properly conducted lobbying.

In any modern society, a **complex and fruitful interaction is constantly happening** between public office holders and various stakeholders. It is now generally accepted that lobbyists can contribute to more enlightened decisions by public office holders since they provide, on behalf of stakeholders, an informed point of view which may merit consideration.

Indeed, lobbying is an intricate part of this interaction between public office holders and the multifarious vested interests or interests groups that compose civil society. In the context of globalisation, lobbyists even attempt to reach and to influence governments from outside their national boundaries.

Any move to regulate lobbying demands the explicit assertion of the legitimacy of lobbying and the setting up of rules and conditions for its proper conduct.

Transparency and standards of behaviour

Existing laws or regulations concerning lobbying have two things in common: the imposition of some degree of transparency and the expression of standards of behaviour with which lobbyists are expected to comply.

In some instances, like at the European Parliament in Brussels, the system works as a **certification procedure** providing those lobbyists who register with privileged access to the premises in which public office holders carry out their activities. Registered lobbyists are required to carry a badge which readily identifies them as the representatives of vested interests or interests groups. As registered lobbyists, they also undertake to abide by a code of conduct.

Such an approach aims at ensuring the appropriate exercise of lobbying on the premises of the governmental or parliamentary institutions. It seems that these requirements for transparency are designed mainly for the benefit of public office holders. It provides the public limited knowledge of the particulars of the lobbying activities happening on the institutional premises and does not seem to reach whatever lobbying activities might be happening outside these premises.

In North America, where lobbying legislation is the rule rather than the exception, transparency requirements for lobbyists stem from the very fact of lobbying a public office holder. These transparency requirements are crafted primarily to inform the public of various particulars of lobbying activities. Statutory provisions and codes of conduct also apply. Such regulations aim not only at informing public office holders on whom they are dealing with, but also, if not primarily, at levelling the playing field with respect to the practice of influence and at increasing public trust in public institutions.[3]

Decision to regulate lobbying in 2002

Even though regulation had been discussed for a few years in Quebec, the decision to regulate lobbying was made in 2002, in the aftermath of a situation involving lobbyists who had deeply embarrassed the government. The Quebec National Assembly then unanimously adopted the Lobbying Transparency and Ethics Act (L.R.Q., Chapter T-11.011). This piece of legislation took inspiration from a federal statute that had been in force since the late 1980s, but in many ways it was more comprehensive and more ambitious in its scope and coverage. It is noteworthy that the framework for regulating lobbying has recently been enhanced in the federal Act. Hence, in the near future, a lobbying commissioner accountable directly to Parliament will be appointed.[4]

The law is **aimed at reinforcing public trust** in public institutions by fostering transparency in the lobbying of public office holders and by ensuring that lobbying activities are conducted properly. Central to this body of rules is a requirement for transparency grounded in the belief that it is in the public interest to know who is attempting to influence the decision-making process of public institutions through lobbying. Statutory provisions governing the practice of lobbying and a code of conduct complete the picture.

The assumptions behind such a statute are that **sufficient knowledge of current lobbying activities** thus made available to the public will create conditions for the democratisation of influence, and that this will positively affect the accountability of public office holders.

Transparency of the substance of their contacts with lobbyists serves as a reminder of the fact that in their decision making public office holders must strike a balance among the interests of various stakeholders, keeping in mind the quest for public interest. It is also expected that, together with these transparency requirements, the setting up of a new ethical framework for the practice of influence will enhance the quality and credibility of the public decision-making processes.

What is to be considered lobbying?

For any attempt at regulating lobbying, **clear legal definitions** of what is at stake in a particular setting are required. Definitions can be a matter of political choice. Three main elements must be defined in order to adequately specify the intended scope of any regulatory process:

- In what political or administrative environment is the regulation to be applied?
- Who is to be considered to be a lobbyist?
- What is to be considered a lobbying activity?

The Quebec law has been quite broad in its coverage of the decision-making apparatus in its public institutions. It encompasses not only the lobbying of ministers, parliamentarians, as well as their staff, but it also covers the lobbying of government employees, the lobbying of persons holding office or employment in government agencies or enterprises, and even the lobbying of elected officials and employees at the level of local authorities.

Two broad categories of lobbyists

The Quebec law defines **two broad categories of lobbyists**, namely:

- consultant lobbyists; and
- "in-house lobbyists" in an enterprise or organisation. In so doing, it should be noted that the law covers not only the action of professional or specialised intermediaries but it also aims at lobbying done directly by and on behalf of enterprises and of organisations.

A **consultant lobbyist** is any person "whose occupation or mandate consists, in whole or in part, in lobbying on behalf of another person **in return for compensation**". This broad category includes individuals acting for third parties in a variety of capacities. Very few individuals have a business card on which they identify themselves as lobbyists. They might be public relations or government relations specialists, project managers, business consultants, former public office holders, lawyers, engineers, architects, accountants and so on. In fact, whatever his or her formal title, as long as a person is lobbying on behalf of another person in return for compensation, that person will be deemed a consultant lobbyist for the intents and purposes of the law.

The second category targets the so-called "in-house lobbyists" whose job or function, within a profit-seeking enterprise or within an association or a non-profit group, consists, for a significant part, in lobbying on behalf of such enterprise or organisation. These might be influential members of the board, executives or other salaried employees of such entities.

Lobbying activities

Having determined that a potential lobbyist is involved in a political or administrative environment covered by the Act, in order for it to apply there needs to be what the law defines as a lobbying activity. Under Quebec law, a lobbying activity implies a direct communication, either oral or written, between a lobbyist and a public office holder. This communication must be made in an attempt to influence a decision-making process in which that public office holder is implicated. It must also relate to any of the subject matters that are enumerated as being susceptible to regulated lobbying.

The Quebec law goes far beyond solely regulating the lobbying of public office holders on their policy making, action plans or the various facets of their legislative and regulatory activity. Attempts by **lobbyists to influence decision-making processes** on more administrative matters such as the issue of administrative authorisations, procurement, the awarding of grants, subsidies or other forms of benefits, even attempts to influence the appointment of senior civil servants may also be deemed to be lobbying activities.

Having somehow defined those three basic concepts which circumscribe its coverage, any effort to regulate lobbying must state which obligations are to be imposed on whom.

Which obligations are to be imposed on whom?

As mentioned before, the regulation of lobbying involves the imposition of some degree of **transparency and the expression of standards of behaviour** with which lobbyists are expected to comply.

As lobbying is a relationship between two actors, a lobbyist and a public office holder, the first question raised concerns which of these actors should bear the formal responsibility for achieving transparency. Since lobbyists initiate the relationship, it is generally assumed that they should be primarily responsible for the publicity of their endeavour to influence public office holders on behalf of the particular or vested interests they represent.

Disclosure at the beginning of a lobbying activity

Typically, and as is the case under the Quebec law, the **filing** of a return in the Registry of Lobbyists is required from the lobbyist in a prescribed delay as soon as the lobbying relationship has started. It is important to note that the filing of that return is not a prerequisite; it is a legal consequence of the beginning of the relationship. Accordingly, public office holders may not be expected to impose the production of proof of registration prior to engaging a relationship with a lobbyist. It shows that registration is not designed as a certification process tantamount to the granting of a licence to lobby. It is essentially conceived as a means to ensure the transparency of the ongoing lobbying relationships for the benefit of citizens and other stakeholders.

This does not mean that public office holders have no role to play in making sure that lobbyists who are at work to influence them abide by the law. Even if the lobbying law does not impose a formal duty on them, public office holders cannot ignore that these requirements are part and parcel of the law of the land. They must show **due and reasonable diligence** in making sure that these requirements are complied with in their dealings with lobbyists. They should bear in mind that transparency requirements imposed on lobbyists in their dealings with them are aimed at enhancing the legitimacy and credibility of their own authority and that they are imposed to ensure an equitable access to the institutional decision-making processes of which they are the trustees and which are designed to determine what is in the public interest.

Table 4.1 and Table 4.2 show the number of new lobbyists registered each year.

Table 4.1. **Trends in the number of lobbyists registered with Quebec's Registry of Lobbyists 2002 to 2007**

Number of new registrations per year

	2002-03	2003-04	2004-05	2005-06	2006-07	2007-08	Total
Consultant lobbyists	91	62	28	28	53	39	**301**
In-house (enterprise or organisation) lobbyists	207	71	58	112	192	388	**1 028**
Total	**298**	**133**	**86**	**140**	**245**	**427**	**1 329**

Table 4.2. **Number of lobbyists with at least one current mandate and numbers of mandates per group of lobbyists in Quebec**

	Number of lobbyists with at least one current mandate as at 31 March 2008	Number of mandates per group of lobbyists
Consultant lobbyists	114	304
Organisation lobbyists	328	487
Enterprise lobbyists	274	197
Total	**716**	**988**

The extent of transparency requirements imposed on lobbyists is a matter of political choice. In a nutshell, the core of required disclosures under the Quebec law could be summarised as "who is lobbying where on what subject matter?".

Identification of parties involved

Who is lobbying refers both to the identification of vested or particular interests attempting to influence public authorities and to the identification of the person or persons acting as lobbyists on their behalf.

Consultant lobbyists must formally **identify themselves** and give their professional particulars. They must also identify in some detail the **client** on behalf of whom they are lobbying. If consultant lobbyists represent various clients, they must file a distinct section of their declaration for each client.

As to lobbying by an enterprise or an organisation, the onus is put on the senior officer of such an entity to properly identify the organisation and to provide its particulars. The senior officer must also duly identify and register the person or persons mandated to act as lobbyists on behalf of the enterprise or organisation.

Regarding where and in which public institution contemplated by the law are the lobbying activities taking place, the requirements are not nominal but of a general nature. In Quebec, lobbyists are not required to identify the person or persons whom they met or intend to meet. It is **sufficient to name the particular institution and identify the nature of the function of the public office holders** they lobby or intend to lobby in that institution. For instance, it is sufficient to mention that one is lobbying at the ministerial or managerial level in a specified ministry or that one intends to lobby members of the board of a specified government agency or enterprise.

Disclosure of subject matter of lobbying

The most essential element of the declaration is a description of the subject matter of the lobbying activities including, as the law says, "particulars to identify such subject matter". This means a **sufficiently detailed description of the nature of the decision that the lobbyist is attempting to influence**. It is noteworthy that the Quebec law does not require the disclosure of lobbying activities as such. It merely requires the disclosure of the subject matter of these lobbying activities.

It might seem at first glance to put a lighter burden on lobbyists. Our experience is that this requirement of particulars as to the subject matter of lobbying activities implies a rather drastic change in the mentalities of those who endeavour to lobby public office holders. Initially, we encountered some reluctance by lobbyists in giving too many details about the purpose of their lobbying activities. Together with the registrar of lobbyists, in order to ensure that declarations are sufficiently detailed, we are gradually developing standards of conformity. Significant efforts were made to reach a relative uniformity in the description of the subject matter of lobbying activities, which is a necessity for the proper working of the Act, particularly for the effectiveness of the "right to know" granted to citizens.

Lobbying techniques and financial resources

The Quebec law asks for very **few details** about how lobbying is to be conducted and also about the financial resources invested to support lobbying activities.

Lobbying techniques are referred to only in the broadest terms such as a general reference to organising or holding meetings, or communicating verbally or in writing. The Quebec law deals strictly with what the literature calls "direct" lobbying as opposed to "indirect" or "grassroots" lobbying which is covered under other jurisdictions. For instance, in Canada, the federal statute requires that indirect lobbying, involving advertisements in the media or public opinion campaigns to influence or to put pressure on decision making by public office holders, be declared.

As to the financial resources invested to support a lobbying drive, the Quebec law requests the disclosure by range of the amount (and not by a specific amount, *e.g.* less than CAD 10 000, between CAD 10 000 and CAD 50 000) of the honoraria paid to a consultant lobbyist. This is quite different from some lobbying legislations in the United States which go quite far in requesting details of the amounts of money invested in a lobbying campaign, as well as the disclosure of political contributions, gifts and other advantages granted by lobbyists to public office holders.

If the Quebec lobbying law might appear timid in that respect, it is no doubt because the same **objectives are pursued by different means**[5] in our legal system. Quebec has quite a **stringent law on the financing of political**

parties. As for gifts and other advantages granted by lobbyists to public office holders, this question is addressed through norms and codes of conduct made applicable to public office holders.[6]

Filing returns and accessibility

Returns are generally filed electronically without a fee on the prescribed form. Those which are not filed in this way are integrated for a fee in the electronic data base of the Registry of Lobbyists. Declaration is an iterative process. For instance, the initiation of any new mandate by a lobbyist must be reported by an adjunction to his initial declaration, as well as any substantial modification in the parameters of a mandate that has previously been declared in the Registry.

Since the purpose of the law is transparency, the content of the Registry of Lobbyists is accessible free of charge to any interested individual at *www.lobby.gouv.qc.ca*.

The Code of Conduct

The second category of obligations imposed on lobbyists concerns the **setting of norms** destined to ensure that lobbying is properly conducted. This is the "ethical", or the "deontological" aspect of the law.

In Quebec, these norms are set either in the law itself, or in the Code of Conduct[7] for Lobbyists which had to be adopted by the Lobbyists Commissioner after consulting the interested parties.

Provisions in the law itself **prohibit** lobbying for a contingency fee or lobbying in return for compensation from a grant or loan from the government. The law also contains provisions that restrict, for a time, the ability of former public office holders of high rank to act as lobbyists in the environment in which they held office. It also contains prescriptions of a more general nature for former public office holders concerning the deriving of undue advantage in lobbying from having previously held public office or the disclosure or usage of confidential information in the course of lobbying activities.

The Code of Conduct for Lobbyists adopted by the Lobbyists Commissioner is in fact a regulation adopted under the law and as such it is compulsory. It establishes standards of behaviour in order to ensure that lobbying activities are properly conducted. These **duties and obligations** are grouped under the headings of "respect for institutions", "honesty and integrity" and "professionalism".

What control mechanisms are to be set up in order to ensure compliance?

In Quebec, it was decided, for very operational reasons, to create both a function of Lobbyists Commissioner and a function of Lobbyists Registrar. There was no compelling reason to do so other than the fact that a specialised team at the Ministry of Justice was already operating some complex computerised registries very successfully. It appeared a sound administrative decision to ask this team to create and operate the Registry of Lobbyists since it had already proven that its members had the know-how and equipment to do the job.

After five years of operation, the Minister of Justice is recommending that the responsibility of operation of the register of lobbyists be **vested with the Lobbyists Commissioner**. According to the Minister, splitting responsibilities under the Act between the Registrar and the Commissioner brings confusion both for lobbyists and for public office holders. According to the minister, having in mind effectiveness, efficiency and accountability, the objective of transparency as defined in the Act would be best achieved by transferring the responsibility for the register to the Commissioner (Ministry of Justice, 2007).

In operating the Registry, the Lobbyists Registrar is responsible for ensuring that returns filed contain all the required information in the manner prescribed. He must also safely safeguard that information and make it conveniently accessible to any interested party.

Simultaneously, the law created the function of Lobbyists Commissioner stipulating that the person holding the office would be "**responsible for monitoring and controlling** the lobbying of public office holders".

Since that institution was to be responsible for monitoring and controlling the relationship between lobbyists and persons holding office in parliamentary, government and municipal institutions, it was decided that the Commissioner would be **appointed on a consensual basis by the National Assembly**, that he or she would be independent from government and accountable directly to the National Assembly to which he or she would report directly and from which the budget would be received.

The Lobbyists Commissioner is granted the powers to **make inspections and inquiries**, both upon request or on his or her own initiative if there are reasonable grounds to believe that there has been a breach of any provision of the Act or of the Code of Conduct. Investigative powers may be exercised with any parties involved, either lobbyists or public office holders.

If the Commissioner's inquiry report ascertains a breach of a provision of the Act or of the Code of Conduct, **various penalties may be requested** against the contravening lobbyist. Fairly substantial fines may be imposed upon conviction by a tribunal.[8] The law also empowers the Attorney General to claim from the contravening lobbyist "the amount or value of any financial or other compensation received or payable to him/her on account of the activities having occasioned the breach". Finally, in cases of grave and repeated breaches of the Law or of the Code of Conduct, the Lobbyists Commissioner might even discipline the lobbyist and bar that individual from lobbying any public office holder for a period of up to a year.

Transformation of lobbying relationship

By imposing transparency in lobbying, this law requires from lobbyists and public office holders alike a very profound change in their way of doing things. It aims at circumventing and at regulating a very diverse and complex reality. It presupposes a **cultural transformation** of the relationship between public office holders and lobbyists. For almost five years, we have approached that task by attempting to strike the right balance between the use of support, incentive and, gradually, coercive measures to ensure compliance.

Our strategic planning was devised with a view to convincing lobbyists, public office holders, and citizens alike to partake in the implementation of the new value system that underlies this bold and recent legislation (Lobbyists Commissioner, 2004).

Fortunately, the National Assembly included a provision in the law to the effect that five years after its adoption, the Minister of Justice would **report on the implementation** of the Act and the Code of Conduct and on the advisability of amending them. The Minister's report was tabled in October 2007 and referred to the Parliamentary Committee on Public Finances.

Anxious to make his contribution to the debate on the basis of experience, the Lobbyists Commissioner filed his own report stating his findings of facts and his recommendations (Lobbyists Commissioner, 2008a; Lobbyists Commissioner, 2008b).[9] This report was also referred to the Parliamentary Committee on Public Finances which studied both reports at the beginning of May 2008. Then the Parliamentary Committee held public hearings and the report of the Parliamentary Committee was tabled.

Assessment of implementation

After five years of implementing the Act, it is fair to say that **nobody contests its relevance, its principles and its validity**, even if one must admit that the Act is still not sufficiently known and many comments are put forth on some specific elements of its implementation.

Our assessment is generally positive.[10] Lobbying activities conducted with parliamentary and governmental institutions are going in the right direction, even if much remains to be achieved. Results are, however, more modest when it comes to the lobbying of local authorities.

Without the firm involvement of public office holders, there is a definite risk that the success of this legislation will be compromised. While by their very nature lobbying activities are not conducted in public but, more often than not, behind closed doors, **public office holders must recognise that this Act gives the citizens, to whom they are accountable, the right to know who is attempting to influence them and on what subject matter**. Since the very purpose of this new "right to know" is to strengthen public trust in the institutions within which they operate, public office holders must reassess their ways of interacting with lobbyists.

If it is not appropriate to formally impose on public office holders the responsibility of making public the information necessary to materialise the transparency requirements of the Act, it is not to say that they have no obligation whatsoever. Because of the very nature and purpose of this Act, we have no hesitation in stating that public office holders have, to say the least, a duty of due diligence with respect to the its observance in their dealings with lobbyists.

As for the more technical elements which will be considered in the process of reassessing the Act, one of the principles is indeed the recommendation by the Minister of Justice that the Lobbyists Commissioner be responsible for the operation of the register.

The most significant of our own proposals for amendment deal with the sanction mechanisms. We recommend that the Lobbyists Commissioner be empowered to initiate by himself or herself the **penal procedures** under the Act. We also ask that the limitation period for penal recourses be extended from one to five years.

Finally, so as to recognise that the cultural changes contemplated by this legislation will not be achieved solely through the use of repressive action, but that they imply the involvement of all concerned, the essential role that the Lobbyists Commissioner must play in **educating all the stakeholders**, be they lobbyists, public office holders or citizens, should be recognised formally in the definition of his mandate.

Conclusions

The OECD 2000 report *Building Public Trust: Ethics Measures in OECD Countries* states that public administrations are not only evaluated on the basis of their ability to reach sound decisions, but also on the **quality and credibility of their decision-making processes**. It advocated the establishment of the components and functions of what it called an "Ethics Infrastructure" that encourages high standards of behaviour and that promotes the integration of values specific to the context of public administration such as impartiality, accessibility, equality, equity and transparency.

In this perspective, the setting up of rules and standards to monitor and control the practice of lobbying might increasingly appear as a **natural complement to the ethical framework** that is put in place to inspire and guide public office holders in the exercise of their functions.

While a few European countries have adopted some form of legislation to control the practice of lobbying (beforehand this was almost exclusively a North American phenomenon), there are growing signs that some more are considering the possibility to do so. The OECD, through its Public Governance and Territorial Development Directorate has been actively involved in reflection on the issue by reviewing experience of developing and implementing regulations for enhancing transparency and accountability in lobbying. Considering the **many efforts to legislate lobbying in the OECD area** and beyond, one might expect that in the coming years, this issue will be studied further, and that international principles or standards might emerge.

In June 2007, the OECD deemed relevant to gather at a Symposium an expert group to review experience and lessons learned in order to develop a framework and principles on lobbying. This framework and principles could shape policy debate and guide decision makers in reviewing and modernising existing arrangements for enhancing transparency and accountability in lobbying.

Notes

1. This chapter was prepared by André C. Côté, Quebec Lobbyists Commissioner.
2. This chapter is based on a paper first presented in March 2007 at the conference "Lobbying: Practice and Legal Framework", held at Sam Son, Viet Nam, under the aegis of the National Assembly of the Socialist Republic of Viet Nam and in June 2007 at the OECD Special Session on Lobbying held by the Expert Group on Conflict of Interest.
3. *Council on Governmental Ethics Laws – COGEL Blue Book: 2006 Lobbying Update on Legislation and Litigation, US and Canada* (document available to COGEL members only).
4. On the same subject, readers may wish to refer to Chapter 3 of this publication, "Canada's Federal Lobbying Legislation: Evolution and Operation of the Lobbyists Registration Act", which was drafted by the Registrar of Lobbyists, Michael Nelson.
5. The Elections Act (L.R.Q., Chapter E-3.3) lists numerous rules regulating political party financing and election spending.
6. See, for example, the Quebec Government's Statement of Values, 21 November 2002, brought before the National Assembly by the Minister of State for Administration and the Public Service and Chair of the Treasury Board. These values are: skills, impartiality, integrity, loyalty and respect: *www.tresor.gouv.qc.ca/fr/publications/ress_humaine/declaration_valeurs.pdf*. For public office holders in Quebec, the following regulations and Acts set out professional obligations: Act respecting the *Ministère du Conseil exécutif*, L.R.Q., Chapter M-30, Article 3.01 to 3.06; Ethics and professional conduct of public office holders, Regulation respecting the R.R.Q., Chapter M-30, r.0.1;

Public Service Act, L.R.Q., Chapter F-3.1.1, Article 1 to 31; Regulation respecting ethics and discipline in the public service, R.R.Q., c-F-3.1.1, r.0.3. Lastly, two Prime Minister's directives published in 2003 set out certain rules on ethics that cabinet ministers and political attachés must observe in order to avoid conflicts of interest, among other things. The key elements of these directives can be found at the following Internet address: *www.premier-ministre.gouv.qc.ca/salle-de-presse/communiques/2003/octobre/2003-10-27.shtm*. In a working document on parliamentary reform brought before the National Assembly on 21 November 2007, the government leader of the House proposes, among other things, the adoption of a code of ethics which would regulate the conduct of deputies: *www.institutions-democratiques.gouv.qc.ca/reforme-des-institutions/documents/document-travail2007-11-21.pdf*.

7. (2004) 7 G.O. II, 1259 [c. T-11.011, r. 0.2]. For further documentation on the Code of Conduct for Lobbyists, see the Internet site of the Lobbyists Commissioner: *www.commissairelobby.qc.ca/commissaire/documentation*.

8. In 2005, the Attorney General of Quebec brought the first proceedings against a lobbyist. This was the very first time such proceedings had been brought in Canada. Since the Act came into force, *i.e.* since 2002, the Lobbyists Commissioner has forwarded to the Director of Criminal and Penal Prosecutions eight inquiry reports into lobbying activities which ascertained breaches of a provision of the Lobbying Act. As a result, seven of these eight inquiry reports ended in infraction notices being served. A guilty plea was entered in three of these cases.

9. Readers may also refer to the list of studies in the annex to this paper conducted at the request of the Lobbyists Commissioner for the five-year review of the Lobbying Act.

10. Some statistics on the Lobbyists Register in Quebec can be consulted in Section 4.3.

ANNEX 4.A1

*Studies Conducted for Quebec's Five-Year Review of the Lobbying Transparency and Ethics Act**

BÉGIN, Luc, *Lobbyisme et titulaires de charges publiques : recommandations pour une responsabilisation accrue*, study conducted with the aid of Steve Jacob, Yves Boisvert, Jean-Patrice Desjardins, Gérard Divay and Serge Belley, Institute of Applied Ethics, Laval University, 18 April 2007.

BELLEY, Serge, Jean-Patrice DESJARDINS and Gérard DIVAY, *Lobbyisme et municipalités – Étude exploratoire réalisée pour le Commissaire au lobbyisme du Québec*, Institute of Applied Ethics, Laval University, 27 February 2007.

COMEAU, Paul-André, *Les sous-ministres et le lobbyisme*, École nationale d'administration publique, August 2006.

DESJARDINS, Jean-Patrice, *Analyse comparée sommaire du rôle des titulaires de charges publiques dans les activités de lobbyisme*, Institute of Applied Ethics, Laval University, 15 December 2006.

DESJARDINS, Jean-Patrice, *La responsabilisation des titulaires de charges publiques en lien avec le lobbyisme*, Institute of Applied Ethics, Laval University, April 2007.

HÉBERT, Martine, *Portrait des activités de lobbyisme au Québec* – Report presented to the Lobbyists Commissioner, May 2007.

HUDON, Raymond, *Dura lex sed lex et Rules are made to be broken – Éclairages sur la Loi sur la transparence et l'éthique en matière de lobbyisme* – Report drafted for the Lobbyists Commissioner of Quebec, May 2007.

JACOB, Steve et Jean-François BÉLANGER, *Les activités de lobbyisme et leur encadrement au Québec : état des lieux et perception auprès des titulaires de charges publiques*, Institute of Applied Ethics, Laval University, 16 April 2007.

* All of these studies can be accessed on the Lobbyists Commissioner's Internet site at *www.commissairelobby.qc.ca* or *www.commissairelobby.qc.ca/promo/97/2*.

Bibliography

Lobbyists Commissioner (2004), Strategic orientations 2004-2007, "Building Trust in our Political and Administrative Institutions", *www.commissairelobby.qc.ca/documents/x_fichiers/628_plan_strategique_04-07.pdf.*

Lobbyists Commissioner (2008a), "Bâtir la confiance – Rapport concernant la révision quinquennale de la Loi sur la transparence et l'éthique en matière de lobbyisme", *www.commissairelobby.qc.ca/documents/File/batir_confiance_rapport_commissaire_lobbyisme_quebec(1).pdf.*

Lobbyists Commissioner (2008b), "L'encadrement des activités de lobbyisme au Québec – Synthèse des activités du Commissaire au lobbyisme du Québec 2002-2007".

Ministry of Justice (2007), "Report on the Implementation of the Lobbying Transparency and Ethics Act and the Code of Conduct for Lobbyists", p. 29.

Lobbyists, Governments and Public Trust, Volume 1
Increasing Transparency through Legislation

Chapter 5

Poland's Experience: Developing and Implementing the Act on Legislative and Regulatory Lobbying[1]

Decision makers in Poland faced a major challenge when defining the scope of legislation on lobbying that would adequately take into account public demands. This chapter outlines the Polish socio-political context under which the government initiated and developed a proposal for legislation on lobbying.

The chapter describes the process in which an original "sanction-oriented" approach to the proposed legislation shifted to a good governance approach that aimed at increasing transparency and accountability in the legislative process. Complementary measures supporting access to public information and consultation in the legislation and law-drafting process are also highlighted.

Moreover, the chapter highlights the government's efforts to implement the new Act on Legislative and Regulatory Lobbying which came into force on 7 March 2006 and provides statistical and qualitative data on the experiences of its application in daily practice.

Summary

Public concerns in Poland about inappropriate lobbying pushed the government to introduce legislation on lobbying in the law-making process. The new Act on Legislative and Regulatory Lobbying was passed by the *Sejm* (Lower House of Parliament) in July 2005 and came into force on 7 March 2006. The Act promotes transparency principally in the law-making process; this is a key step to improving transparency in the entire public administration and all legislation.

This chapter describes and analyses the **critical views on "lobbying practices" in the social and political context of the country's transition process**. The draft law submitted to the *Sejm* in October 2003 evolved substantially over time. During debates in the Extraordinary Committee, the aims and approach of the draft law on lobbying shifted from a focus on "policing and punishing misbehaviour" to promoting principles of good governance, in particular transparency and accountability. The chapter reviews major **elements of the new legislation**, such as:

- its scope, that is the definition of "lobbying activities", and the types of lobbyists covered;
- procedures for registration and disclosure; and
- sanctions in case of breaching the Act.

The chapter also presents **implementing measures** required of the public administration to put the new provisions into effect, such as publicising legislative work programmes and organising public hearings. In particular, it highlights the procedures for registering lobbyists and provides statistical data on the reporting of lobbyists.

The Ministry of the Interior and Administration, which is the central body in charge of administering the Act, launched a **survey** to review and report on implementation and practice. Survey results (see Annex 5.A1) provide insights on the level of preparedness in the central government administration and on the impact of new legislation. The results also reveal remaining challenges and indicate possible measures to overcome these challenges.

The socio-political context

The social and political context of Poland's transition process is particular, and the **Polish people have perceived lobbying very negatively**. Research consistently demonstrated that all too often lobbying in Poland has consisted of networks of informal connections, through which private interests, on the basis of "reciprocity of mutual services", penetrate the contacts between business groups and the political elites. "Access to the relevant decision maker" is considered "key capital". And when economic circumstances have worsened and opportunities based on market potential have slid, then such "access to key decision makers" only increases in significance.

Contacts with such public officials may be "earned" in various ways. Indeed, relationships between the worlds of business and politics in Poland are often based on unethical practices; the most effective method of "arranging" the settlement of issues consists of kickbacks.

Research confirms inappropriate lobbying practices

Research commissioned by the National Chamber of Commerce (KIG) in 1998 revealed that local councillors believed that one out of three politicians "accommodated" the interests of a particular firm and conducted "business prospecting" on its behalf, as part of his or her official public activity. That same study showed that members of Parliament believed the number to be almost one out of four politicians. In a report on corruption in 1999, the World Bank described the **"pathological" forms of lobbying** in the *Sejm* (Lower House of Parliament), as including the practice of providing financial benefits in return for the "favours" of blocking or modifying the provisions to be included in laws (World Bank, 2000).

According to research by the Philosophy and Sociology Institute at the Polish Academy of Sciences[2] (IFiS PAN) dating from 2000, as many as 28% of MPs surveyed in their third term of office in the *Sejm*, pointed at corrupt and "corruption-provoking" methods as the most frequently used **methods of exerting influence** upon the members of Parliament. These methods included:

- trading in influence (*i.e.* proposals of seats on supervisory boards of business companies);
- bribery or bribery attempts;
- illegal donations;
- funding of expensive "gifts" (such as, cars for "testing");
- personal benefits (providing "attractive services", sponsoring "attractive excursions" or "study travels"); and
- promises of financing of electoral campaigns and cash contributions to party funds.

Research conducted in 2004 by the Stefan Batory Foundation showed that as many as 35% of all Poles and 19% of Polish parliamentarians believed that bribery may effectively lead to the repeal of a legislative Act or a change in the law. In the same year, the Public Opinion Polling Centre (CBOS) conducted a similar survey, the results of which showed that 69% of the Polish people thought that cash could be successfully used to have an impact on the drafting of legislation.[3]

Very few people working in co-operation with Parliament in the legislative process would admit that they actually practise the profession of lobbying. Law offices, consulting firms and public relations agencies **frequently act as "covert" lobbyists**. At Parliamentary committee meetings, people from these firms appear in the roles of "experts" or "advisers", surprisingly enough acting in the capacity of experts on behalf of political parties or deputies, rather than as representatives of third-party stakeholders. As a consequence of this untransparent practice, the law-making process may suffer from the dubious impact of particular vested interests.

"Rywin's affair" spurs proposed lobbying legislation

The "Rywin's affair",[4] which uncovered a number of **irregularities in the law-making process**, led to the drafting of a proposal for a legislative Act on Lobbying. The case revealed that there was no public disclosure required, nor any kind of social control over the process of drafting of legal regulations. The details of the affair indicated clearly that in the course of developing a law, the influences of various private circles were more important than the public interest. Moreover, it turned out that such influences could result in high-value "commissions", sometimes millions of dollars.

The "Rywin's affair" and the ensuing inquiries of the Parliamentary Investigation Committee demonstrated to the political class and to society at large that **it was essential to regulate the "lobbying business"** through the law. This became more pressing as a series of other corruption affairs involving politicians and public servants in charge of developing laws, on the one hand, and professional lobbyists, on the other, saw the light of day Such cases unveiled repeated incidences of voluntary assistants of MPs and high ranking officials in the public administration acting in practice as lobbyists and promoting the interests of their clients.

It was under such circumstances that the government of Prime Minister Leszek Miller submitted a draft law on lobbying. However, the same government later offered its own resignation under the pressure of allegations of corruption and involvement in dubious business dealings.

Redefining the draft law on lobbying: The Parliamentary process

Over a period of nearly two years, the **draft law on lobbying evolved from a focus on "sanction" to a focus on greater transparency** through public disclosure. On 28 October 2003, the *Sejm* received the government's draft law on lobbying activities. On 12 November 2003, during the *Sejm* session, a motion to dismiss the Bill on lobbying was rejected by a clear majority of votes; the Bill was submitted to an Extraordinary Committee. After several Committee meetings, in which expert opinions were reviewed and numerous amendments were brought, the Extraordinary Committee[5] sent the Bill back to the *Sejm* and recommended its adoption. On 7 July 2005, the *Sejm* passed the Bill with 399 votes in favour, four abstentions and no votes against the new law. The upper chamber of Parliament adopted the text as proposed by the *Sejm*. On 15 August 2005, the President of the Republic of Poland signed the final Act on lobbying activity in the legislative process, referred to hereafter to as the "Act on Lobbying".[6]

The Extraordinary Committee's work

The Extraordinary Committee started its work in January 2004, and a new bill was elaborated based on the ideas of the government's draft law. As mentioned earlier, the original draft law submitted by the government was very restrictive, and was geared "**to seek out and punish misbehaviour**" (as one of the experts defined it).

Business associations had a number of **concerns about the draft law**. Amongst their statutory objectives is s lobbying on behalf of their members. Members' contributions serve as a sort of "fee" for such activities. The business community strongly demanded that the draft law should specify *expressis verbis* that the Chambers of Commerce and Industry are bodies whose rights cannot be infringed upon by the law. These business associations also requested that the same arrangement apply to all non-governmental organisations. The basis for such claims was that the draft law on lobbying ruled out the possibility of lobbying activities being conducted by political parties, and therefore, by analogy, the Chambers of Commerce and Industry (as organisations of entrepreneurs) should also be excluded.

Indeed, the original draft law specified **what groups and organisations were not subject** to its requirements. It listed representatives of diplomatic missions, political parties, trade unions, as well as associations of employers.

As a result of the work of the Extraordinary Committee, the list of exclusions was abandoned and was replaced by **positive statements** contained in Article 2 of the adopted Act:

- For the purposes of the Act, lobbying means any legal action designed to influence the legislative or regulatory actions of a public authority.
- For the purposes of the Act, professional lobbying means any paid activity carried out for or on behalf of a third party with a view to ensuring that their interests are fully reflected in legislation or regulation proposed or pending.

- Professional lobbying can be carried out by a firm (hereinafter referred to as the professional lobbying firm) or by an individual not registered as such (hereinafter referred to as the professional lobbyist) pursuant to a civil law contract.

Efforts of the Business Centre Club and MPs of the Law and Justice Party

Such changes were the result of the efforts of the Business Centre Club (BCC) and other employers' organisations, and also the convictions of a number of deputies active on the Extraordinary Committee, as well as their political parties. These changes – considered by several experts to be definitely positive – gave rise, however, to a number of critical comments, which are presented later in this chapter.

A number of prominent MPs from the Law and Justice Party (PiS), who later formed a coalition government, had strongly opposed the draft law submitted by the government.[7] Subsequently, their representatives who took part in the work of the Extraordinary Committee had a major impact on amendments that produced an **evolution in the approach** of the Bill. Finally, in 2005, the Law and Justice Party unanimously supported the adoption of the Act on Lobbying in the law-making process.

Representatives of the BCC actively took part in the work of the Extraordinary Committee. The BCC was one of a select few organisations involved in representing employers' organisations and the business community. The BCC issued an opinion that pointed out a number of deficiencies in the initial draft law. While the BCC recognised the need for legal regulation of lobbying activities and to improve transparency, it found the Bill excessively restrictive, allowing for arbitrary decisions by public officials. The BCC criticised the Bill for being "policing oriented" as well as on the determination of which firm or persons were to be regarded as conducting lobbying activities The Parliamentary Extraordinary Committee on the Bill accommodated the criticisms and comments made by the BCC.

Local self-government authorities

Another issue under debate concerned whether or not to include local self-government authorities in the scope of the law on lobbying. In the discussions on the Bill, voices were raised that lobbying also exists in decision making at the sub-national level, and that territorial self-governments should not be excluded from the scope of legislation. It was agreed, however, that **local laws have a different nature** than the legislation adopted at the central level. Yet, it was noted that transparency of decision making at the local level should not be diminished.

Ultimately, the newly adopted law on lobbying **does not require territorial self-governments to disclose the programmes of their legislative work** to the public (as is the case with the Council of Ministers and other central authorities). Nevertheless, the territorial self-government was not excluded from the sphere of lobbying activities.

As part of the work of the Extraordinary Committee, the expert studies noted the fact that the "public authority" by definition also comprises the territorial self-government, so the provisions referring to public authorities are **also applicable to the sub-national level of administration**. This also concerns Article 14, which refers to the right to conduct activities on the premises of public bodies, and Articles 15, 16 and 17 dealing with the co-operation between lobbyists and organs of public authority. In addition, Article 18, which requires representatives of a public authority to provide information about lobbying activities conducted with respect to such bodies, also covers territorial self-governments.

However, the units of territorial self-government are not required, according to the Act, to disclose their legislative plans to the general public (Articles 3-8), it therefore follows that the provisions on "public hearing", described in Articles 8 and 9, do not apply to local authorities.

Box 5.1. **Evolution of the Polish Bill on Lobbying in the Parliamentary debate: Summary of changes**

The essential changes proposed by the Extraordinary Committee and later adopted by the *Sejm* and Senate concerned the underlying **orientation** of the Bill; **it shifted from a restrictive, sanction-oriented approach towards promoting good governance** through enhancing transparency of the legislative process. On the one hand, the new Act provides access to the legislative process for persons and firms interested in influencing that process; and, on the other hand, it requires public disclosure of any attempt to influence law making. The government's initial draft law aimed at controlling the bodies undertaking lobbying activities, including businesses, political parties, business organisations and NGOs. The fundamental change in approach, which is supported by MPs and experts, shifted the emphasis from controlling the bodies undertaking lobbying activities to increasing transparency and accountability in the public administration.

No restrictions *per se* were imposed on legitimate lobbying activities, nevertheless, any person or firm carrying out lobbying activities must publicly disclose information on such operations, including information on who is being represented and the regulations being targeted. These changes to the law should definitely support greater transparency in lobbying activities and prevent people from taking advantage of informal relationships. Sanctions imposed upon those conducting unregistered lobbying activities should also help reduce the informal influencing of public officials.

Key elements of the Act

The Act describes the principles of conducting lobbying activities. **"Lobbying activities" consist of actions conducted by legally admissible methods that seek to influence public authorities in the law-making process**. Lobbying activities aim to ensure that the arguments and interests of social and professional groups are taken into account in the decisions of public officials. Lobbying may also be practiced by organisations and associations with the objective of protecting and promoting the interests of their members.

Professional lobbying activities

The Act also introduces the notion of "professional lobbying activity", that is, lobbying on behalf of other persons in exchange for money. As construed in the law, professional lobbying activities consist of gainful lobbying activities conducted on behalf of third parties for pursuing their interests in the law-making process. Professional lobbying activity may be exercised on the basis of a civil law contract by an entrepreneur or by a physical person who is not an entrepreneur.

Register of professional lobbyists

Entities conducting such activities must communicate details about themselves to the relevant publicly-accessible Register. The Minister of the Interior and Administration is required to keep such a Register of legal entities professionally conducting lobbying activities.

Sanctions

An entity which performs professional lobbying activities without entering them in the Register shall be subject to a fine ranging from PLN 3 000 to PLN 50 000.[8] Such a sanction is to be imposed by way of an administrative decision by the Minister of the Interior and Administration. Determining factors for the level of the monetary penalty are the degree of influence of the lobbyist on the decision of a public authority, as well as the scope and nature of professional lobbying activities undertaken by the entity. It is possible to impose the monetary fine repeatedly, if the professional lobbying activities were continued without due entry in the Register.

Legislative work programme

At least once every six months, the government shall prepare and publish on the website of the Public Information Bulletin (BIP) the programme of legislative work concerning draft laws. This legislative work programme will also indicate any end to the work on a given draft law, along with the reason for such a halt. Similar programmes of legislative work should be prepared and published on draft ordinances. These plans are to be drawn up by the Council of Ministers, the chairman of the Council of Ministers, and by the individual ministers. Draft laws and ordinances should be disclosed in the BIP once they have been transmitted for co-ordinating consultations with the members of the Council of Ministers.

Public hearing

After publication, anyone shall be able to submit "notification of interest" (on an official form) in the work on the draft laws or ordinance to the body responsible for the preparation of such a draft. Such notification shall also be published in the BIP. Subsequently, the notifying party shall be able to present an opinion concerning the specific draft during the "public hearing".

The body responsible for preparing a draft ordinance shall be able to conduct a public hearing on the draft. Information concerning the timing of the public hearing on a draft ordinance shall be made available in the BIP at least seven days prior to the date of that public hearing. Any party which has submitted its interest in the work on the draft ordinance at least three days before the date of the public hearing shall be entitled to participate in the public hearing.

A public hearing on a bill already introduced to the *Sejm* is to be conducted in accordance with the principles specified in the procedural rules of Parliament. In such a case, a party that had submitted its notification of interest in the work on the Bill shall be able to participate in the public hearing on the draft.

Information on personnel supporting law-making

Important provisions of the new Act include requirements to furnish information on assistants and voluntary assistants of parliamentarians and ministers, employees of political cabinets of ministers and staff of the parliamentary caucuses. Indeed, amendments have been introduced to the following Acts: the Act of 9 May 1996 on the performance of the mandate of deputy and senator; and the Act of 8 August 1996 on the Council of Ministers. Leaders of the parliamentary caucuses, deputies and senators, as well as ministers, are now required to **publicly disclose the following information** on their collaborators, mentioned above:

- first, middle and last names;
- date of birth;
- places of employment over the three-year period preceding the date on which the person became an employee of the office of a parliamentary caucus or political group, or a voluntary collaborator;

- sources of income over the three-year period preceding the date on which the person became an employee of the office of a parliamentary caucus or political group, or its voluntary collaborator; and
- information concerning the business activities undertaken during the three-year period preceding the date on which the person became an employee of the office of a parliamentary caucus or political group, or its voluntary collaborator.

Steps required of the government administration to implement the Act

The Extraordinary Committee developed the main duties that the public administration would need to undertake in relation to the **implementation of the Act** in order to ensure full transparency of legislative activities. The administration needed to fulfil the following:

- Firstly, the Council of Ministers and the particular ministers needed to prepare the governing principles related to the drafting and public disclosure of the **programmes of legislative work**. Such programmes must be prepared at least once every six months and be disclosed publicly in compliance with the requirements of the Act on Access to Public Information. Any changes occurring within the domain of public information must be disclosed within 24 hours in the electronic BIP. As a consequence of these requirements, the chairman of the Council of Ministers and ministers had to prepare decrees imposing such duties upon the ministries and specifying the modes of procedure, as well as naming the competent organs in charge of execution of such duties. It was deemed helpful if the same format of public disclosure of legislative programmes were applied at all public bodies.
- Secondly, internal orders to regulate the **mode of co-operation with lobbyists on the premises** of public administration had to be implemented, in line with Article 14 of the Act that allows the performance of lobbying activities on the premises of public administration and requires the heads of public offices to grant access to rooms and appropriate representation of interest groups.
- The *Sejm* and Senate had to introduce appropriate changes in order to specify their **rules on the performance of lobbying activities on their premises**. The progress of legislative work undertaken in both chambers of Parliament is publicly disclosed and accessible on their respective websites.
- A key task for the Minister of the Interior and Administration was the creation of **the Register** of firms conducting lobbying activities, with rules and procedures, document formats for the Register, and the model certificate that confirms the registration of lobbying firms on the Register.

- The heads of particular ministries and public authorities were also required to prepare and approve the procedures on the **publication of information** disclosed by public offices on lobbying activities within the scope of their competencies.

Before the Act entered into force, a number of additional aspects remained to be regulated by the public administration. For example, developing rules to determine whether particular actions are indeed regarded as lobbying activities, so as to **avoid uncertainty** amongst both public officials and those conducting lobbying activities. The Act required the Minister of the Interior and Administration to issue an ordinance on the registration form for submissions to the Registry, while the Council of Ministers had to issue an ordinance specifying the procedure for the notification of interest in the work on a draft law or ordinance, including a format of the notification form.

It was also necessary to **develop procedures for public disclosure** of information provided by the entrepreneur. Any person conducting lobbying activities is obliged to inform the public authorities in a written statement that indicates the entities and clients on behalf of which he or she is conducting lobbying activities. The Presidium of the *Sejm* had to amend the *Sejm's* Rules of Procedure, so as to regulate the whole procedure of work on bills, starting from the time of receipt of a proposal and ending with the actual adoption of the final legislative act.

The Rules of Procedure of the *Sejm* and the implementation of executive provisions of the public administration also had to specify the mode of conduct by chairpersons of parliamentary committees and heads of public offices as they preside over **public hearings on legislative acts** and other legal acts. The Act on Lobbying only mentioned the institution of public hearing without specifying the way in which it should be conducted and documented.

All the requirements listed above had to be implemented by 7 March 2006, the date of entry into force of the Act.

These three steps – two one-off activities and one to be carried out annually – could support a better understanding of how the new Act functions and what improvements are necessary.

Box 5.2. Evaluating the effectiveness of the Polish Act on Lobbying and its implementation: Proposed steps

As lobbying was a new field of legislation, it would be useful to evaluate the effectiveness of the Act and its implementing mechanisms. The following three steps could provide a framework for evaluating the new Act on Lobbying:

- Consult the public on their opinion with the aim of identifying good and bad practices. Such consultation could support and improve not only the law, but also the implementing decrees regulating the activities of public administration.
- Review lobbying activities and criminal cases related to the new law and actual lobbying practices. A review should be carried out annually and the results presented to the Minister of the Interior and Public Administration.
- Consult with the representatives of local self-governments on lobbying practices at the sub-national level and prepare a report on the findings.

New Act on Lobbying: Critical views and challenges

The Act on Lobbying in the law-making process adopted by the *Sejm* provoked doubts and criticism amongst the Polish public. But reactions were often contradictory. The principal and most serious criticism related to the **limited scope of the Act**. Namely, it established a subjective list of legislative institutions, which are obliged to be open to lobbyists; but for unknown reasons the list did not include the Office of the President of the Republic of Poland. Another criticism with regards to the Act concerns the **insufficient control measures** applicable to lobbying activities. Control is handled by officials of the same institutions where lobbying activities take place. According to the critics, such a solution can lead to "excessive discretion", lacks uniformity of control criteria, and represents a serious risk of exposure to conflict of interest.

The Association of Professional Lobbyists in Poland criticised the Act, saying it was drafted too rapidly, and that some of its provisions reflect outright **wishful thinking** (*e.g.* the enigmatic provision stating that the heads of public offices are obliged to assure appropriate conditions for the conduct of lobbying activities).

Provisions concerning the **public hearings** organised by the ministries also seem rather "unfortunate". Article 9 Paragraph 4 states that if "... due to constraints of the available rooms, in particular owing to the number of persons wishing to participate in a public hearing, it is not feasible to organise a public hearing concerning a draft regulation, the entity entitled to its organisation may: [...] cancel the public hearing, disclosing the reasons behind such cancellation in the Public Information Bulletin". This provision might provide opportunities for irregularities, owing to the fact that it enables the ministries to avoid a public hearing.

The Polish Confederation of Private Employers *Lewiatan* (Leviathan), which groups a number of major business enterprises in the country, stated that the regulation adopted by the *Sejm* does not resolve the problem of corrupt lobbying, as it does not grant active lobbyists such rights as to motivate them to leave the "shadow economy". According to the authors of the statement, only **balanced duties and rights** on the part of entities performing professional lobbying activities, extending beyond the scope of the rights to which each and every citizen is entitled to by virtue of the law, can contribute to the elimination of the "grey zone" in the environment of lobbyists.

Indeed, the newly introduced regulation **ought to eliminate the phenomenon of pathological lobbying, connected with corruption**, and the use of informal connections at the interface between politics and business. The newly created regulation should motivate representatives advocating particular interests to conduct their activities in an open manner in compliance with the law, by means of vesting them with rights and privileges obtained in connection with the undertaking of lobbying activities in a way compliant with the new regulations.

Entities conducting lobbying activities, as defined in the various provisions of the law, should by virtue of the law **have guaranteed access to information** of interest to them, contact with public officials, the right to participate in consultative conferences, sub-committees and committees of the *Sejm* and Senate, as well as the right to attend plenary sessions of Parliament. Such privileges ought to balance, if not outweigh, the duties imposed upon the entities conducting lobbying activities and should extend beyond the rights granted to any other entity by virtue of the law.

Need for lobbyists' self-regulation

The Constitution of Poland and the rights stemming from the provisions of the Act on Access to Public Information already provide every Polish citizen with broadly defined rights concerning freedom of information. Only by granting entities performing lobbying activities with relatively wide ranging and distinct privileges will the "grey zone" of activities be weakened, and the "economic viability" of conducting lobbying activities in an open and official manner improved. Provisions going in this direction ought to be reinforced by **self-regulation of professional practitioners** of lobbying activities. Lobbyists, out of their own self-interest and motivated by the need to gain esteem for their activities and the confidence of the wider public, should be interested in purging existing pathologies and negative connotations associated with "lobbying". The Act adopted by the *Sejm* does not meet the assumptions noted above. The only clearly specified right granted to entities conducting professional lobbying activities consists of the entitlement to participate in public hearings, which may not necessarily be organised by the body responsible for the specific draft law.

Social partners should be recognised

The Act completely disregards the issue of **social partners**, whose legitimate entitlement to take part in the law-making process is **undisputable and deeply rooted in the Polish system of developing laws**. Those bodies, by virtue of the law, participate in the process of consultation on provisions of the law, expressing their opinions and taking actions intended to achieve specific results. Thus, they conduct lobbying activities, but the rights associated with this stem from other regulations. These social partners have demonstrated over the years strong and positive contributions to the process of consulting on laws now enacted. It is not without justified reason that they are regarded as an important and inalienable element of social reality, vital for the proper functioning of the democratic state. Social partners, due to their own mode of conduct of activities should be recognised as entities conducting lobbying without remuneration, and therefore the same Act should reinforce their rights (although in the sphere of duties their social position and motivation should not be considered the same as those entities professionally practicing lobbying).

Non-governmental organisations

Representatives of non-governmental organisations (NGOs) pointed out a number of problems connected with the threats to which their activities were exposed by the Act on Lobbying. According to some experts, the distinction between professional and non-professional lobbying activity only theoretically resolved the problem of NGOs, which would not wish to be treated in the same way as commercial lobbyists. NGOs which would like to occasionally lobby in favour of specific legal provisions have not been made subject to any additional registration, control or other requirements stemming from the Act, nor are they covered by the provisions requiring the heads of public offices to facilitate lobbying activities. Theoretically, therefore, NGOs not acting in the capacity of professional lobbyists do not enjoy the right to conduct lobbying activities on the premises of public offices and cannot count on their assistance.

In addition to the fact that the definition of lobbying is considered imperfect (it very generally defines lobbying as any kind of "activities leading to exertion of influence upon the bodies of public authority in the course of the law-making process"), it might suddenly turn out that the "soft advocacy of interests", for example, on the occasion of the work on the Act on Activities for the Public Benefit and Voluntary Activities, might now be included in the scope of professional lobbying activities and might require the hiring of professional lobbyists by non-governmental organisations. There were signs that representatives of non-governmental organisations were unwelcome at some of the Parliamentary committee meetings and by certain deputies. There were reasons for concern that the Act on Lobbying in the law-making process might provide a pretext for the limitation of the already rather insignificant role of NGOs in the law-making process. Therefore, according to some independent experts, it is hard to determine with any certainty, whether the Act on Lobbying in the law-making process will in the future obstruct or assist these organisations in their dialogue with public institutions.

Insufficient time between the Act's adoption and entry into force

The first challenge for implementation of the Act on Lobbying in the law-making process was the short interval between its approval and its entry into force. The question was to what extent the Polish public administration could manage to prepare on time all the appropriate procedures and ordinances necessary for the implementation of the tasks imposed upon it by the Act.

Role of social and business organisations needs clarification

The role of social and business organisations in the context of lobbying activities needs to be defined clearly. The public administration, as well as circles of entrepreneurs, and non-governmental organisations need to each play a part in this clarification. The role of the media in public communications cannot be overestimated in this regard. There is no doubt that lobbying should be absolutely open and transparent, and it should also be subject to social control.

Identification badges for increased transparency

Some experts pointed out that in spite of the existence of a public Register of lobbying firms that in instances of lobbying there may be no clear indication if someone is indeed a lobbyist. It might be necessary to apply the same rules as those already existing in other countries or the European Parliament, for example, the requirement to wear appropriate identification badges.

Ensuring more open and transparent lobbying activities

In spite of a number of critical remarks against the Act on Lobbying in the law-making process, there is no question as to its substantial value and significance for combating corruption and enhancing transparency of activities of public administration. At the present stage, the primary aim is to ensure the efficient functioning of the public administration on the basis of the adopted Act. Ensuring implementation and assessment of its functioning is much more important than any further amendment of existing legal regulations.

Finally, a very positive aspect of the Act merits being underlined: it will **support a professional approach to lobbying activities** – without creating a closed group and at the same time definitely strengthening the professional community of lobbyists. Thanks to this Act, all the activities based on personal connections and "peculiar" arrangements between the worlds of politics and business ought to be eliminated.

As the "Lobbying Act" strictly aimed at the preparation of laws, many experts noticed that the new Act made no mention of the public administration and consider that a mistake. The answer to this seems quite simple. However, for a balanced view the following should be taken into consideration:

- First, the "Lobbying Act" **was a response tailored to public outcry following the corruption affairs** described in the first part of this chapter.
- Second, the primary aim of the new Act was to **make the law-making process more transparent**. It does not regulate lobbying activities in other areas. Those areas are regulated by other Acts, such as the Public Procurement Law,[9] the Anti-Corruption Law,[10] the Criminal Code,[11] etc. The Extraordinary Committee took the view that it was better to make improvements in a specific area rather than to try to improve everything simultaneously.

Register of entities conducting professional lobbying activity

A critical element of the implementation of the new Act was the **development of the Register by the Ministry of the Interior and Administration**. The Register is regulated by the Act on Lobbying and the Regulation on the Register of entities conducting professional lobbying activity, hereinafter referred to as the "Regulation".[12] The objective of the Register is to promote transparency of professional lobbying activities and the entities carrying them out.

The Register is public, and the information contained – with the exception of addresses of physical persons – is available on the Internet site of the BIP of the Ministry of the Interior and Administration at *www.mswia.gov.pl*. Those entities conducting professional lobbying activities are required to register through an official form.[13] The application can also be submitted in paper form using a computer printout or an official registration form. **The following data must be included in the application:**

- company name, corporate seat and address of the entrepreneur conducting professional lobbying activity or the first name, last name and address of a physical person who is not an entrepreneur conducting professional lobbying activity;
- in cases where the entrepreneurs are conducting professional lobbying activities, the number in the Register of Entrepreneurs of the National Court Register or the number in the Register of Economic Activity;

- current extract from the Register of Entrepreneurs of the National Court Register or current certificate of entry into the Register of Economic Activity – in case of entrepreneurs conducting professional lobbying activity;
- proof of payment of PLN 100 for entry into the Register, or its certified copy containing data indicated on the application should be additionally added to the application;
- certified copies of identification papers in the case of non-entrepreneurs who are conducting professional lobbying activity under a civil law agreement; and
- if applicable, power of attorney is needed in order to submit the application form or other documents constituting a basis for representation of the entity entered into the Register.

The application must be signed by the applicant or their representative seven days after the application was submitted, unless the application has formal deficiencies or is unfounded. **The Register provides the following data:**

- serial number entry;
- date of entry into the Register and dates of any further modifications;
- company of the entrepreneur conducting the professional lobbying activity or the first name and last name of a physical person who is not an entrepreneur conducting such activity;
- corporate seat and address of the entrepreneur or address of the physical person;
- national Court Register number in the Register of Entrepreneurs or, in the case of entrepreneurs conducting professional lobbying activity, the number in the Register of Economic Activity;
- date and grounds for removal from the Register;
- file reference number; and
- comments.

Separate files are kept for every registered entity entered into the Register. Up to August 2009, 141 entities conducting professional lobbying activities had been registered. In case of formal deficiencies on the application, the authority keeping the Register requests the applying entity to remove them. Failure to remove the formal deficiencies within seven days results in an administrative decision refusing entry into the Register. Refusal shall also be issued if the application is obviously groundless. Up to August 2009, formal deficiencies were found in certain applications, and the applying entities were requested to remove them. Moreover, 17 administrative decisions **refusing entry into the Register** were issued, because of:

- No obligation to enter into the Register. In four cases, non-profit organisations not conducting economic activity were refused from registration.

- Formal deficiencies in the application of entry to the Register. In two cases, the applications were not adequately filled out.

In case of modifications in data entered, the entities submitting applications to the Register are obliged to report these changes within seven days of their occurrence. In the second half of 2006, only one entry update was performed in the Register.

Upon request of entities submitting applications to the Register, the authority administering the Register issues a **certificate of entry into the Register**,[14] which remains valid for three months from the day it was issued. Up to 1 December 2006, all 75 entities registered requested certificates of entry into the Register.

The entity application is also a necessary condition for removing this entity from the Register. Removal from the Register in the form of an administrative decision is also issued by virtue of a final and binding decision prohibiting professional lobbying activity conducted by the entrepreneur or a physical person.[15] An entity can be **removed from the Register** pursuant to:

- cessation of professional lobbying activity; and
- binding final decision of the court prohibiting the execution of professional lobbying activity.

As at 1 December 2006, no entity had been removed from the Register.

In case of professional lobbying activity (as defined by the Act) conducted by an entity not entered in the Register, the competent public authority is obliged to immediately inform the Minister of the Interior and Administration. The Act also anticipates **penal and administrative sanctions** for lobbying by unregistered entities. The administrative decision of the Minister of Interior and Administration can impose a fine of up to PLN 50 000. As at 15 June 2008, no fine for unregistered professional lobbying had been imposed.

Implementation and enforcement: Survey results and future steps

Six months after the Act on Lobbying in the law-making process came into force, a questionnaire was sent out to all ministries as well as the Chancellery of the Prime Minister in November 2006. **The questionnaire had three aims**, namely to review:

- the **preparedness** of government administration for implementing the tasks imposed by the Act on Lobbying in the law-making process;
- the number and nature of **lobbying measures** undertaken in the ministries; and
- **challenges** to the enforcement of the Act and possible areas for improvement in the Act on Lobbying in the law-making process.

By the end of 2006, all ministries and the Chancellery of the Prime Minister had provided their answers. The questionnaire used in the survey can be found in Annex 5.A1. Table 5.A1.1 presents the **answers to** all questions, except question number five that collected information on inquiries with the prepared legal acts submitted by persons and organisations that are not professional lobbyists and provide information concerning the legal acts of their interest. The full list of entities involved in the legislative process can be found in the following table.

Table 5.1. **Inquiries of lobbyists related to law making in Poland**

No.	Ministries	No. of inquiries linked to legislative work	No. of inquiries of professional lobbyists
1	Chancellery of the Prime Minister	3	–
2	Ministry of Finance	5	1
3	Ministry of Agriculture and Rural Development	3	–
4	Ministry of National Education	–	–
5	Ministry of Foreign Affairs	–	–
6	Ministry of Regional Development	–	–
7	Ministry of the Treasury	–	1
8	Ministry of Construction	–	–
9	Ministry of Labour and Social Policy	1	–
10	Ministry of Sport	5	–
11	Ministry of Transport	–	1
12	Ministry of Health	3	–
13	Ministry of Science and Higher Education	–	1
14	Ministry of National Defense	–	–
15	Ministry of the Environment	2	–
16	Ministry of Culture and National Heritage	1	–
17	Maritime Economy Ministry	–	–
18	Ministry of Economy	1	1
19	Ministry of Justice	4	–
20	Ministry of Interior and Administration	–	–

The survey results confirmed that not all central government ministries introduced internal regulations for official procedures related to contact with lobbyists, despite the statutory obligation resulting from Article 16 (2) of the Act on Lobbying in the law-making process. The following ministries had not yet introduced appropriate regulations by mid-December 2006:

- Ministry of Justice.
- Maritime Economy Ministry.
- Ministry of National Defense.
- Ministry of Sport.

- Ministry of Construction.
- Ministry of National Education.

Internal regulations aim at determining both the actions undertaken in the legislation process and the principles of conduct when lobbyists contact public officials. Some of these internal regulations – such as banning all contacts with lobbyists outside the office building – seem obvious; however, it is necessary to express them in law in order to introduce comprehensive actions for enhancing transparency.

The fact that **only five entities conducting professional lobbying** activities reported to ministries at the end of December 2006 is considered **surprising**. In comparison with 75 entities registered with the Ministry of the Interior and Administration, this modest amount of actions undertaken by professional lobbyists raises considerations of targeted offices. An analysis of institutions could constitute a basis for a possible amendment to the Act on Lobbying in the law-making process. In particular, the considerable number of inquiries related to legal acts by entities which are not professional lobbyists should be noted.

Draft legal acts are usually presented in publications of drafts and justifications as required by the Act on Lobbying in the law-making process. However, persons responsible for administering the BIP need to pay more attention in ensuring that **detailed information about employees of the ministry's political cabinet** is in line with Article 22 of the Act. For example, information needs to be provided not only on employees' financial assets, but also on the place of work or economic activity in the last three years before holding public office.

Analysis indicated that government administration was **generally prepared for implementing** the tasks required by the Act on Lobbying in the law-making process. Sufficient attention should be drawn to certain deficiencies such as unfamiliarity with and incomprehension of the Act as well as implementing regulations. These deficiencies clearly hinder the proper enforcement of the Act. Survey results make the following **recommendations**:

- Introduce **internal regulations** for implementing the Act on Lobbying in the law-making process in all ministries; in many cases there are no detailed principles for contacts with professional and non-professional lobbyists.
- Provide **sufficient capacity** for offices in charge of task implementation imposed by the Act on Lobbying in the law-making process, as these tasks are often time-consuming and interfere with other tasks.
- **Ensure uniform interpretation** of the Act on Lobbying in the law-making process. Survey answers that indicate doubts would constitute the basis of developing such an interpretation.

- Develop a **standardised model based on good practices** for presenting required information for publishing information in the BIP. There are clear deficiencies in the obligation imposed by the Act to publish information on the legislative process.
- Prepare **training programmes** on lobbying and implementing tasks resulting from the Act on Lobbying in the law-making process; conducting such trainings mainly among the managerial staff of the offices in charge of implementing the Act.
- Develop **procedures for contacts** of public information officers with lobbyists (both professional and non-professional ones) based on tasks resulting from the Act on Lobbying in the law-making process.
- **Optimise procedures** where already implemented, by comparing them with those used in other offices and selecting good practices.

Reports on the implementation of the Act

Analysis of the survey results, together with control questions and inter-departmental consultations, indicated the necessity to prepare a new and a **more complex version of the report on the enforcement** of the Act on Lobbying in the law-making process. The first survey did not cover the lobbying phenomenon as a whole and only focused on efforts of ministries and the Chancellery of the Prime Minister. In addition to enforcement of the Act, future reports should also include other government organisations and the preparation of annual reports on lobbying should provide an effective monitoring tool for public authorities. In line with Article 19 of the Act on Lobbying in the law-making process that imposes the collection of information on contacts with professional lobbyists until the end of February every year, it seems reasonable to change the deadline for the preparation of the annual report on lobbying from the second into the first half of each year. This would allow using collected information and studies in annual reports.

Although criticism of the Act on Lobbying in the law-making process has been repeatedly expressed in the media and professional discussions; **no one questioned the necessity to enter the legislation on lobbying into force**. To make the most of possible future modifications, they should be preceded by **careful preparations**, including:

- careful analysis of findings and recommendations prepared in the annual report on lobbying;
- extensive consultations with public administration offices, professional lobbyists, civil society organisations and lawyers on lessons learned in implementing the Act on Lobbying; and
- ensuring the consistency of any possible amendments of the Act with governmental strategies for modernising the state administration.

Notes

1. This chapter was prepared by Juliusz Galkowski, Anti-Corruption Strategy Co-ordination Group, Public Administration Department, Ministry of the Interior and Administration, Poland.
2. *www.ce.uw.edu.pl/wydawnictwo/Kwart_2002_4/Jasiecki.pdf.*
3. *www.batory.org.pl/english/corrupt/bar.htm.*
4. The Rywin's affair is the most well-known corruption affair in Poland that initiated an inquiry by the Special Parliamentary Commission. It is named after the businessman Lew Rywin, who offered his help to change the "Media Law" in return for a large bribe. He said that he stood on behalf of "the group of people who are ruling". After the "Rywin's affair", corruption was ranked as the fourth biggest "national problem" of Poland.
5. The Extraordinary Committee is a special body of the Polish Parliament. Usually ordinary committees work on all drafts, but if the Bill is complicated or needs more attention, the *Sejm* can establish an Extraordinary Committee with a single purpose to work only on this specific Bill.
6. *Journal of Laws*, No. 169, item 1414.
7. In 2003 the Parliamentary caucus of this party voted in favour of dismissing the draft law.
8. EUR 1 is approximately PLN 4 (fines range from EUR 750 to EUR 12 500).
9. *http://isip.sejm.gov.pl/prawo/index.html.*
10. *www.abc.com.pl/serwis/du/1997/0679.htm.*
11. *www.mswia.gov.pl/index.php?dzial=57&id=1793.*
12. Regulation of the Minister of the Interior and Administration of 20 February 2006 on the register of entities conducting professional lobbying activity, *Journal of Laws*, No. 34, item 240.
13. The standard form is published in Annex No. 1 to the Regulation.
14. This certificate of entry into the Register is a standard form published in Annex No. 2 to the Regulation.
15. Pursuant to Article 41 of the Penal Code or Article 9 (1)(5) of the Act of 28 October 2002 on Liability of collective entities for prohibited acts subject to punishment, *Journal of Laws*, No. 197, item 1661 as amended.

ANNEX 5.A1

Survey on the Implementation of Poland's Lobbying Act

Table 5.A1.1. **Questionnaire on the implementation of the Polish Act on Lobbying**

Below is the survey questionnaire submitted in November 2006 to those ministries listed in Table 5.A1.2.

1. Were there any special lobbying-related procedures introduced in your office?
   Please describe them.
2. Were the following items prepared and published in the Public Information Bulletin:
   a) Legislative work programme.
   b) All documents connected with legislative works.
   c) Inquiries connected with legislative works.
   Please list all inquiries connected with legislative works.
3. Which unit in your office is responsible for preparation and publication of documents connected with legislative works?
4. Did any professional lobbyists report to your office?
   If yes, please indicate (pursuant to Article 18 of the Law):
   a) In which matters were the lobbyists interested.
   b) Specification of professional lobbyists.
   c) Determination of forms of undertaken activity (supporting a specific project, opposing projects, proposed changes, etc.).
   d) Determination of impact which the actions undertaken by the lobbyists had on the prepared drafts.
5. Please list the inquiries with the prepared legal acts submitted by persons and organisations that are not professional lobbyists and provide information concerning the legal acts of their interest.
   At the same time please provide information about:
   a) Forms of undertaken activity (supporting specific projects, opposing projects, proposed changes, etc.).
   b) The impact of the actions undertaken by lobbyists on the prepared drafts.
6. Were there any public hearings in the matter of prepared legal acts conducted in your office?
7. Did any questions or doubts connected with the following issues emerge in course of work conducted by the office:
   a) Register of the prepared acts.
   b) Register of inquiries.
   c) Presentation of information on the Internet.
   If yes, please describe them.

Table 5.A1.2. **Survey results on implementation of the Polish Act on Lobbying**

Ministries	Questions					
	1	2	3	4	5	6	7
Chancellery of the Prime Minister	Yes	*a)* Yes *b)* Yes *c)* Yes	Competent units are responsible for preparing drafts. The Governmental Information Center is responsible for their publication.	No	–	No	No questions.
Ministry of Finance	Yes	*a)* No *b)* No *c)* Yes	Joint organisational units – making documents available, Public Information Bulletin editor in every department – publication of documents.	Yes	–	No	Should the Law on State Treasury guarantee be published in the Public Information Bulletin?
Ministry of Agriculture and Rural Development	Yes	*a)* Yes *b)* Yes *c)* Yes	Organizational unit – responsible for preparation of documents, The General Director's Office – is responsible for publication of documents.	No	–	No	No questions.
Ministry of National Education	No	*a)* Yes *b)* Yes *c)* No	Departments and Offices within the Ministry of National Education – are responsible for preparation and publication of documents, Information and Promotion Office of the Ministry of National Education.	No	–	No	The questions referred to the necessity to publish in the Public Information Bulletin documents concerning the prepared drafts of legal acts. There are doubts regarding which documents fall under the term "all documents".
Ministry of Foreign Affairs	Yes	*a)* Yes *b)* Yes *c)* No	General Director's Office	No	–	No	The question referred to the moment, when the obligation to share documentation connected with works on draft international agreement in specific process in which they are concluded emerges as well as to the scope of the shared documentation.

Table 5.A1.2. **Survey results on implementation of the Polish Act on Lobbying** *(cont.)*

Ministries	Questions						
	1	2	3	4	5	6	7
Ministry of Regional Development	Yes	*a)* Yes *b)* Yes *c)* No	The person responsible for Information and Promotion in co-operation with appropriate competent departments responsible for preparation of draft legal acts.	No	–	No	No questions.
Ministry of the Treasury	Yes	*a)* Yes *b)* No *c)* No conducted Internet site update works.	Competent department – is responsible for preparation of documents, Secretariat of the Minister and Regional Offices Co-ordination – is responsible for publication of documents.	Yes	–	No	Questions emerged with respect to the method in which the applications are registered and regarding the procedure of handling persons who do not conduct professional lobbying activity yet inquire in connection with works on draft normative acts.
Ministry of Construction	No	*a)* No *b)* Yes *c)* No	All units within the scope of their activities.	No	–	No	No questions.
Ministry of Labour and Social Policy	Yes	*a)* Yes *b)* Yes *c)* Yes	Individual departments.	No	–	No	No questions.
Ministry of Sport	No	*a)* Yes *b)* Yes *c)* Yes	The Department of Law and Control – forwards documents for publication, the Office of the Managing Director – is responsible for substantive contents.	No	–	No	No questions.
Ministry of Transport	Yes	*a)* Yes *b)* Yes *c)* No	Appropriate competent organisational units.	Yes	–	No	No questions.
Ministry of Health	Yes	*a)* Yes *b)* Yes *c)* Yes	Appropriate organisational unit of the Ministry of Health – is responsible for preparation of documents, the Press and Promotion Office is responsible for publication of documents.	No	–	No	No questions.

Table 5.A1.2. **Survey results on implementation of the Polish Act on Lobbying** *(cont.)*

Ministries	Questions					
	1	2	3	4	5	6	7
Ministry of Science and Higher Education	Yes	*a)* Yes *b)* Yes *c)* No	The Office of the Minister, Department of Information and Promotion.	Yes	–	No	Explanation of the term "all documents concerning works on the draft"; Does this imply also internal documents, which were prepared prior to publication of the draft in the public information bulletin? Does this imply documents connected with reported interest of external entities on works performed in relation to the project?
Ministry of National Defense	No	*a)* Yes *b)* Yes *c)* No	The Law Department is responsible for publication of documents, The Information Center of the Ministry of National Defense – is responsible for preparation of documents.	No	–	No	No questions.
Ministry of the Environment	Yes	*a)* Yes *b)* Yes *c)* Yes	Competent units – are responsible for preparation of documents, the Department of Education and Promotion of Sustainable Development – is responsible for publication of documents.	No	–	Yes	Yes: there is no determination of time limit for publication and time limit for removal of the posted materials from the Public Information Bulletin in the Law. There is no record concerning the form in which the materials should be provided, in order to post them on the pages of the Public Information Bulletin, as materials submitted as hard copies require typing in or scanning, and these activities are time-consuming.

Table 5.A1.2. **Survey results on implementation of the Polish Act on Lobbying** *(cont.)*

Ministries	Questions						
	1	2	3	4	5	6	7
Ministry of Culture and National Heritage	Yes	*a)* Yes *b)* Yes *c)* Yes	The Department of Law and Legislation – is responsible for preparation of documents, the General Director's Office – is responsible for their publication.	No	–	No	No questions.
Maritime Economy Ministry	No	*a)* No *b)* Yes *c)* No	Impossible at this stage.	No	–	No	No questions.
Ministry of Economy	Yes	*a)* *b)* *c)* Yes	Person appointed by the Department Director – the so-called Legislator is responsible for a given draft legal act, and departmental editors are responsible for their publication.	Yes	–	No	No questions.
Ministry of Justice	No	*a)* Yes *b)* No *c)* No	Appropriate organisational unit responsible for development of draft legal acts, Legislative and Legal Department is the unit responsible for editorial and legislative preparation. The Office of the Minister is responsible for supporting the Public Information Bulletin.	No	–	No	No questions.
Ministry of Interior and Administration	Yes	*a)* Yes	Appropriate organisational unit of the Ministry or an organisational unit of the department – is responsible for preparation, publication, announcement of normative acts. Office of the Minister of Interior and Administration – is responsible for publication of documents.	No	–	No	A question was submitted by the Polish Chamber of Liquid Fuels concerning explanation of the statutory activity conducted by the Polish Chamber of Liquid Fuels in light of the Law; questions also emerged with respect to presentation of information on the Internet.

Bibliography

World Bank, "Anti-Corruption in Transition. A Tribute to the Policy Debate", 2000.

OECD PUBLISHING, 2, rue André-Pascal, 75775 PARIS CEDEX 16
PRINTED IN FRANCE
(42 2009 19 1 P) ISBN 978-92-64-07336-4 – No. 56971 2009